JESUS,
the
GIFT of LOVE

JESUS,
the
GIFT *of* LOVE

JEAN VANIER

CROSSROAD • NEW YORK

1994

The Crossroad Publishing Company
370 Lexington Avenue, New York, NY 10017

Copyright © 1994 by Jean Vanier

Printed in the United States of America

Library of Congress Cataloging-in-Publication Data
Vanier, Jean, 1928–
    Jesus, the gift of love / by Jean Vanier.
        p.   cm.
    ISBN 0-8245-1415-7
    1. Jesus Christ—Biography—Devotional literature.   I. Title
BT306.5.V34   1994
232.9'01—dc20
    [B]   93-46879
                                                                    CIP

*I want to thank the following people
who took time to read the manuscript
and who gave me some very precious advice:*

> Rev. Frances Young
> Canon Donald Allchin
> Rev. Nicholas Hudson
> Rev. Jock Dalrymple
> Rev. David Wilson
> Sue Mosteller
> Claire de Miribel
> Sr. Stanislas Kennedy
> Br. Roland Walls
> Anne Osler
> Rev. Gerald O'Collins
> Rev. Philip Kearney
> Rev. Henri Nouwen
> Bella Feliciano
> Xavier Lepichon
> Gilles Lecardinal

*I would like to give special thanks to Anne King,
who worked on the text to make it better.*

CONTENTS

INTRODUCTION _____

I write this book as a follower of Jesus.
I left the navy in 1950
in order to respond to a gentle call of Jesus
to leave all and follow him.
Since then I have tried to walk with him,
to learn little by little
the secrets of the universe
and even more,
the secrets of God.
I have tried — so often unsuccessfully —
to live and to love and to speak
as he lived and loved and spoke
and to struggle against the powers of evil
in and around me
as he struggled with the powers of evil around him.

The yearnings of Jesus
are the yearnings of love for people
just as they are
in all their poverty and brokenness,
with their masks and systems of defense,
in all their beauty too.
His yearnings are that we as human beings,
each one of us
no matter how "little" or "big,"
may reach fulfillment
and be filled with the ecstasy of living.
His yearnings are to undo the chains

that bind us up in guilt and egoism
and prevent us from walking on the road
to inner freedom and growth.
His yearnings are to liberate
the deepest energies hidden within us all
so that we may become men and women of compassion,
peacemakers
like him,
not fleeing the pain and conflict
of our broken world,
but taking our place in it,
building up community and places of love
and thus bringing hope to our world.

Yes, I write this book
so that his love and healing power
may be revealed more to young and old alike
and above all to those who do not know Jesus,
those who are suspicious of him
and of the Church he founded.

For many years I have tried to be a follower of Jesus.
I have tasted this joy and growth to freedom.
But I have struggled too.
I have touched my own mediocrity and ambivalence,
letting myself sink into the quagmire
of my own fears
and desires for control and comfort;
my fear of rejection,
of being dishonored,
seen as guilty,
condemned by others.
I have touched the vulnerability of my heart
and the troubled waters of emptiness and anguish.
I have protected this vulnerability
through my own defense mechanisms and angers,
and various forms of flight.

I write this book to reveal the immense goodness of Jesus.
There is no harshness in him,
no urge to control others or to impose his will on them.
He is not there to make people feel guilty
or to pass judgment on them.
He is motivated by a sense of mission.
He is strong
and in him resides the light of truth,
a deep humility,
and the innocent love of a child
calling,
waiting,
to give life.
Jesus, the gentle lover and healer,
calls each one of us
to fullness and to life,
quietly penetrating the darkness of our world
— our inner and outer world —
disturbing us in our pride, fear, and blockages
in order to call forth the light
in each of us.

This book then is the story of Jesus
as it is revealed in those four books
called the Gospels,
written by Matthew, Mark, Luke, and John.
My hope is that this book
will lead people to the words and gestures of Jesus
given in them.
The Gospels are the Word of God
given to us by the Holy Spirit,
who inspired those four men.
They either witnessed themselves
the events they speak of
or were informed by such witnesses.
They wrote these books some time after the events
so that we might believe in Jesus

as he was and lived.
Clearly oral tradition was not enough.
It was important to put the story down in writing.
And each one, in his own unique way
and according to his purpose
and the people for whom he was writing,
blended facts, interpretation of facts,
and symbolic meanings
as well as interpretations of Scripture.

I have used the four Gospels
but have tried to bring them together
into one meditation on the story of Jesus,
using events, extracts that seemed particularly significant,
in order to understand not only
the public, external life of Jesus,
but also his inner life.
I realize that each one of the written Gospels
had its own perspective, choice of events,
and interpretations
in order to bring the message to a particular audience.
Bringing the four Gospels together into one story
obliges me to leave out
what is specific to each one.
It has the advantage, however,
of giving a more unified story and vision
of the life of Jesus,
of who he is and why he came
and what he brings to our broken humanity.

I am aware, of course,
that the Gospels give rise to many questions, such as:
— when exactly were these books written?
— what are their exact sources?
— the basic texts we have are in Greek:
    what were the real words of Jesus in his own language?
    Are the words we have a true translation of the Greek
    or an interpretation?

—what is the exact chronology of the life of Jesus?
— how does one explain certain discrepancies
    in points of detail among these four books?

I do not seek to answer these questions or others.
It is not my purpose in this book.
All I know is that whatever the questions
there is a marvelous convergence and coherence
among these four books.
Together they give a clear portrait of Jesus
as he was and as he lived,
a clear vision of his message.
From his conception to his death and resurrection
we see a man manifestly sent by God
to reveal God,
to point a way of universal love, of truth,
of justice and of peace;
a man endowed with special powers,
strikingly free,
speaking with authority,
totally humble,
loving people
yet disturbing them,
coming in a special way
to announce good news
to the poor, the lowly, the weak,
and the crushed of humanity.

I write this book as a follower of Jesus
to reveal Jesus as I know and love him
and as I am loved by him.
It is not then the work of a scholar,
an erudite historian,
or a well-versed exegetical student.
Such people are needed and are important,
but that is not my calling.
This book is the work of a man
who has, of course, his blind spots and inadequacies,

but who wishes only to pass on
what has been given to him.
Today I read these Gospels that have nourished my life
and inspired my vision of humanity
in quite a different way than I did forty years ago.
I read them with my mind and heart
formed and transformed
by my years of living
faithfully and unfaithfully
with the risen Jesus;
formed and transformed
by my contact with my spiritual father,
Thomas Philippe,
and my contact with many others,
especially with those who are poor and weak and in need.
I have also been nourished
by other well-documented lives of Jesus or commentaries.
This work is impregnated by my own life,
by my own maturity and immaturity
as a follower of Jesus.

I have tried to remain close to the actual words
of the Gospels
though not always giving the references
so as not to make the text too heavy or academic.
This book is not meant to be a textbook
but rather a meditation.
Those who know the Gospels will quickly recognize
the words and phrases taken from them.
Those who do not know them
will, I hope, find them as they grow
to read and to love the Gospels themselves.

Occasionally I interpreted the Gospels
without seeking to back up my interpretations
in order to maintain the simple style of a book
announcing good news.

I want to depict the true Jesus as he was,
not the one I want him to be.
So I continue to search
and to listen to those who are more scholarly
or more enlightened or holy than I.
I ask to be enlightened
and to be purified of illusions
by the Spirit of Jesus.

Some of my interpretations flow obviously
from my knowledge of human beings,
from the anthropology I have learnt over the years
and the knowledge I have
of the importance of the mother-child relationship
in the development of a person towards maturity.
For some thirty years now
I have been living in l'Arche
with men and women who have learning difficulties,
sometimes with severe disabilities.
They are weak and powerless people
but amazingly open and trusting.
Jesus came to announce good news
to the poor and the lowly
and these people are clearly among
the poor and the lowly.
The Gospel is truly good news for them.
So they have taught me a great deal about Jesus,
who he is,
what his message is,
how to open my heart to him
like a child.

They have revealed to me in a special way
the weakness and the meaning of human flesh,
and thus the meaning of the Word made flesh
and his downward path
into weakness and vulnerability.
With them I have lived an experience of communion;

I have discovered how communion —
the to-and-fro of love between hearts —
is the fundamental experience of every human being,
the origin of all human development
and of the growth of love and compassion.
It can become the place of grace,
a presence of God.
These men and women transmit love
not just by words
but by gestures of love
through their flesh.
It is in these gestures of love
that I have discovered communion
and how Jesus transmits love and communion
not just by his words
but also through his flesh, his body.

L'Arche was founded in 1964 when,
inspired by Father Thomas Philippe
I welcomed Raphael and Philippe,
two men with mental handicaps,
from a rather dismal institution
to live with me in a small house in Trosly-Breuil, France.
From this initial community
one hundred others have been born
with the same vision and inspiration.
Each community is made up of a number houses
and, when necessary, workshops and schools.
People with mental handicaps
and those who come to live with them
live together in small houses
inserted into a local area.
In l'Arche we are discovering work, prayer,
forgiveness, and celebration;
we minister to each other
and celebrate our being bonded together,
our oneness.

❈

As I grow to know Jesus today
risen from the dead,
living and loving in my heart
through faith and love,
inspiring believers all over the world;
as I grow in the knowledge of human beings
and of my own humanity;
as I read history,
particularly the history of two thousand years ago;
as I deepen my understanding and love
of the four Gospel books
I see no opposition between the living Jesus of today
and the historical Jesus
revealed in time, in history, and in the Gospels,
revealed essentially by those who witnessed his life
and his love.
He is one and the same.
If we love him,
all his gestures and words in time are vital,
as vital as all that is revealed
in our hearts today about him
through the Holy Spirit,
and all that is revealed in the history of the Church
over time,
for it is the one, same, living Jesus.
Jesus as he lived in Galilee and Judea
is our model;
he actually said that he washed his disciples' feet
as an *example* for us.
We, his followers,
are called to live and to love
as he lived and loved,
to imitate all that he is,
not externally
but internally,

inspired as he was by the Holy Spirit,
in union and in communion with the Father.
The Gospels are there not just to lead us to belief,
the belief that he is living in us today
and in the Church,
but to teach us how to live and to act
in our broken world today.
That is why John, the beloved disciple, says
in the letter he wrote to his community:

> "Those who say they abide in Jesus
> ought to walk as he walked." (1 John 2)

I offer this book for those like me
who are yearning for life,
for meaning,
for inner liberation,
and who wish to walk as Jesus walked,
to live as he lived
under the guidance and inspiration of his Father,
continually in communion with the Father,
and with other followers of Jesus,
and with others who are searching
for peace,
for love,
and for truth.

I

THE BEGINNINGS ___

At the Time of Jesus

Roman troops had invaded Palestine
some sixty years before the birth of Jesus.
According to their cunning policy,
the Romans appointed local rulers,
frequently weak people seeking self-glory.
They gave them privileges and power,
as long as they remained vassals of the emperor.

And so it was that Herod, the one they called "the great,"
became King of Judea
some forty years before the birth of Jesus.
Herod was a vicious and lustful man,
prepared to make all kinds of compromises
with his Roman masters
and use all forms of cruelty to maintain power
and build up his name, fame, and fortune.
He was not a man of faith
but a dictator filled with his own self-glory
who imposed order and a certain prosperity
through terror.
The Romans knew how to make good use of him
to serve their interests and power.

In Matthew's Gospel (Mt 2)
we are told how in a rage

he sent out soldiers and police
to kill all the babies under two
in Bethlehem and the surrounding district,
hoping in this way to eliminate the Christ,
the prophesied King and Pastor of the people of Israel
whose birth had been announced by wise men
coming from the East.
Can there be a more horrible, vicious crime
against humanity?
The blood of babies staining their cradles
and flowing on the roads of Bethlehem,
their tiny bodies mutilated, cut up by swords,
thrown into ditches;
mothers screaming their pain,
fathers, brothers, uncles clenching their fists,
containing anger, revolt, inner rage, desire for revenge
but also feelings of helplessness, anguish, powerlessness
in the face of evil
and the power of the sword.

The Romans, masters of the universe,
knew that they were the greatest people of the earth,
the epitome of culture, knowledge, technology,
science, and wealth.
They despised the insignificant people of Palestine,
the Jews,
with their "fanatical" religious ways,
their strange dress and rituals,
their belief in one God,
their ignorance and petty theological squabblings.
The Romans governed through fear and cruelty.

Crushed and humiliated by these pagans,
the Jews submitted more or less angrily,
knowing they could do nothing against such power.
Some sought to make the best
out of an impossible situation:
accepting conditions, playing safe,

maintaining a certain freedom
in order to live their Jewish laws and rituals
and comply with the call of God.

Some Jews benefited from the Roman presence,
collaborating with the Romans,
making money,
renouncing their Jewish faith, at least in public;
this was the choice not only of the publicans,
the tax collectors, and other money-making people,
even women victims of prostitution and wine merchants,
but also of all those who were around Herod's court,
his army and courtiers.
Many drowned their fears and humiliation
in drink and loose living,
trying to forget all their shame and inner pain.

Others, in the name of religion
and pride of culture and race,
created rebel groups,
freedom fighters,
terrorists seeking revenge.
They resorted to violent resistance,
stabbing soldiers,
those whom they saw as the vassals of Satan,
desecrating the holy name of God.
They sought to create the right conditions
for armed rebellion.
In all their zeal and courage
they hoped to restore the Kingdom of Israel
through violence and the power of God.
They were called "Zealots."
Such a rebellion actually did take place in Galilee*
not long before the birth of Jesus,
under the leadership of a man named Judas,
son of Ezechias.

---

*See Daniel Rops, *Jesus and His Times* (Buccaneer Books, 1990), ch. 3.

Varus, the Roman legate in Syria,
quelled the rebellion
and in retaliation, with two legions,
crucified two thousand men.
In his Gospel, Luke refers to men of Galilee
who were killed by the troops of Pilate in the Temple:
their blood mixed with the blood
of sacrificed animals (Lk 13).
Among the Jewish people, particularly in Galilee,
hatred of the Romans, their cruelty and domination,
was always ready to erupt in revolt.

The high priest was the religious leader of Israel;
he was assisted by a multitude of priests.
And there were the scribes, the doctors of the Law,
men versed in the Torah.
The Sanhedrin was a sort of senate or council of elders
composed of seventy-one men:
the high priest, other priests, scribes, and elders.
It was like a supreme council of the government,
a tribunal,
and also a place of theological discussion.
The high priest carried quite a bit of power
in this religious society,
but he was highly controlled by the occupying forces,
the Romans,
who nominated him and used him for their purposes.

Among the Jews were the Pharisees,
who formed a sort of pious fraternity,
the "separated ones," the "holy ones."
They were generally lay people, artisans.
They had come into existence
two or three centuries previously.
When the Jewish people in all their humiliation
became more conscious of their lack of faith and love,
they realized that they had to change
and to turn back to the Law of God:

"Be holy as God is holy."
To be "holy" meant to be "different,"
faithfulness to the Law of God and purity.
Obedience to the Law of God
would preserve their Jewish identity.
For centuries Israel had been under the domination
of Babylon, Persia, Greece, and now the Romans.
Since many pagan foreigners in their land had brought in
new ways, customs, and economy,
the Jews were in danger of losing their identity.
Obedience to the obligations of the Law,
and particularly those concerning everyday realities
of food, meeting people,
what to do or what not to do on the Sabbath day,
gave them a sense of being set apart from foreigners
and enhanced the sense of their own identity
as the chosen ones of God.

It was the role of the scribes, on the other hand,
to formulate all the requirements of the Law.
There was something noble and great
in their love of the Torah.
Some were truly prayerful
as were some of the priests who served in the sanctuary.
Others, however, had become scrupulously obsessed
with the observance of the minute details of the Law,
forgetting the heart of the Torah:
adoration of the Lord their God,
and compassion, love of neighbor.
Like many other religious groups in the course of history
they sought to preserve their own identity
and maintain spiritual power
more than to serve the Lord in love.

Many of the Jewish people
were proudly jealous of their identity,
their "holiness,"
their being "chosen by God";

they were intolerant of the pagans,
those who worshipped idols.
The Jews clearly divided the world
into the pure and the impure,
the good and the bad.

The Sadducee party, on the other hand,
was made up of the more conservative,
wealthy land owners
and of many priests;
they clung to the most ancient Hebrew traditions
and rejected all novelties of belief or ritual.
More than the Pharisees,
whom they did not like,
they sought a compromise with the Romans
in order to maintain their power and wealth
but also their Jewish ways.
As in all such situations,
some were sincere, honest, pious;
others, fearful of conflict or persecution,
were profiting from their power and wealth
in order to live a comfortable life.

Among the Jewish people of that time,
there was a small wealthy class,
the land owners,
there were the artisans and merchants,
and then there was the majority of the people,
poor and lowly:
simple folk, some very pious,
others unlearned in the things of the Law.
Some were day workers, hired by the wealthy,
living from day to day;
others lived off the land.
As in many cultures, in all times,
the wealthy and the learned often scorned the lowly.
In John's Gospel it is said
that some Pharisees spoke of them

as "the crowd ignorant of the Law
and who are cursed" (Jn 7).
Others respected them and saw them as the *anawim*,
the poor of the Lord.

Many of the rich and the powerful looked down upon
all the beggars, the lepers, the crippled,
those with severe handicaps,
as if they were punished by God.
They were seen as impure, dirty, evil,
cut off from God
and the things of God.
They had no voice in Jewish society
and no place in the Temple.
They lived in disgrace;
there was no grace, no value in them.
Many, filled with anguish,
felt guilty for existing,
crying out their pain.
Some would flee into mental illness
and forms of despair,
drudgery, and disgust of self;
they felt there was no hope for them,
only damnation,
in this life, and in the next.

Other Jewish people, however, faithful to the prophets
and particularly Isaiah
saw them as neighbors to be cared for with compassion.

> "Is not this the sort of fast that pleases me:
> to break unjust fetters,
> to undo the thongs of the yoke,
> to let the oppressed go free
> and to break all yokes?
> Is it not sharing your food with the hungry
> and sheltering the homeless poor;
> if you see someone lacking in clothes,

to clothe him
and not to turn away from your own kin?"

(Is 58)

Some of the Jews were called sinners;
they could not or did not fulfill the Law.
Among them were the tax collectors, called publicans,
hated by the Jews,
looked down upon
because they collaborated with the Romans,
and women, victims of prostitution
who sought out a living
from the Roman troops,
hungry and greedy for affection.
The Roman camp was at Magdala,
on the Lake of Tiberias,
and as in all countries where there are foreign troops,
prostitution developed nearby.

Many of the Jewish people, however,
believed in Yahweh,
prayed the psalms fervently,
read the Torah,
and continued to put their hope in Yahweh.
They were the *anawim,*
the poor of Adonai.
They frequented the Temple,
offered sacrifices,
prayed daily to the Lord,
and yearned for the coming of the Messiah.

"I lift up my eyes to the hills;
From whence does my help come?
My help comes from the Lord
who made heaven and earth.

"He will not let your foot stumble;
he who keeps you will not slumber.

Behold, he who keeps Israel
will neither slumber nor sleep.

"The Lord is your keeper;
The Lord is your shade
on your right hand.
The sun will not smite you by day,
nor the moon by night.

"The Lord will keep you from all evil;
he will keep your life.
The Lord will keep your comings and goings,
from this time forth and forevermore." (Ps 121)

Near Jericho there was a group of men called Essenes,
who lived a strict, ascetic life in community,
totally separated from the rest of the people.
They had cut themselves off from the Temple
and all the rituals.
They were waiting for the coming of the Kingdom,
in adoration
and in a rigid, even harsh, community life,
without mercy or acceptance of others.
The Gospels do not speak of these men,
but we know about them
through the discoveries of the Dead Sea scrolls,
found in a cave near Jericho in 1946.

John the Baptist (Mt 3, Mk 1, Lk 3, Jn 1, 3)

It was into this confused and conflictual situation,
where anger and despair were smoldering,
that a man called John appeared.
He was a prophet.
There had been no prophets in Israel
for many years;
this made some people feel as if Israel
had been abandoned by God,

though others were still living in expectancy,
waiting and hoping for something to happen:
the end of the world?
the end of a world?
the coming of the Messiah,
the "one who is to come" to restore the Kingdom?

John dressed like a prophet,
in camel's hair,
not with the flowing garments of the Pharisees.
John ate like a prophet, locusts and wild honey.
John cried out like a prophet,
shouting the word of God with all its force and truth,
its simplicity and directness,
issuing severe warnings:
if people did not change their ways,
if they did not repent,
they would be punished,
eaten up by fire.
The end of the world?
The end of a world?

He cried out to the Pharisees and Sadducees:
"brood of vipers!"
warning them not to consider themselves an elite of God
but to change their hearts
and the direction of their lives.

Many people came from Jerusalem
and all the surrounding districts
to be washed by John
in the waters of the Jordan,
confessing their unfaithfulness to God
and the evil they had done.
He called all to a change of heart.
He did not tell them to become Zealots
and to struggle through violence,
nor to obey the minute regulations of the Law.

He did not ask people to change externally—
— if they were soldiers or tax collectors
they should remain as they were—
but to change internally.
He cried out for repentance,
a change of heart.
He called people to compassion,
to share with the poor,
inspired certainly by the prophet Isaiah:

> "Let those who have two tunics, give one away
> to those who have none;
> and let those who have food do likewise." (Lk 3)

Above all,
John announced that "another is to come" after him;
John was but "a voice crying out in the wilderness"
attributing to himself
the words of the prophet Isaiah (40:3)
to prepare the way of the Lord.
This other would baptize
not with water as he did,
but with the Holy Spirit and with fire.
John said he was not even worthy
to undo the straps of the sandals
of the one who was to come,
who was unknown to the leaders,
unknown to the people,
unknown even to him, John,
until the Spirit of God
in the form of a dove
descended upon this other.

This other was Jesus.
He came and knelt humbly before John
in the waters of the Jordan,
asking to be baptized by John
who recognized him then
as the Son of God,

the Messiah,
the one who was to come,
the one for whom he was called to prepare the way.
As he baptized Jesus
John heard a voice from Heaven saying:

> "This is my Son, my Beloved,
> in whom I am well pleased."

From then on John cried out:

> "He must increase
> and I must decrease."

John was a cousin of Jesus,
and the son of Zechariah and Elizabeth,
conceived miraculously
when Elizabeth was already old in age.
But he had not known that Jesus, his cousin,
was the "one who is to come."

The role of a prophet is always to announce the truth,
the word of God,
without any quibblings or complexities;
it is to show the way to life and to liberation
in the face of all the powers of evil, of unfaithfulness,
of illusion, of lies, and of death.
John called for a conversion of the heart;
he pointed to Jesus and announced
that he was the way.
Once the prophet has shown the way,
he can disappear;
his work is done.
John pointed to Jesus
and then disappeared.
Because he had announced the truth
and the ways of God,
he was imprisoned by Herod Antipas,
the son of Herod the Great,

who was reigning over Galilee at the time.
Herod did not want to hear what John had to say.
He was a cruel and lustful man, like his father.

One night at a large party (Mk 6),
when he was drunk with wine and lust,
he made a wild promise
to the beautiful daughter of his "wife," Herodias,
who hated John with rage
for he had denounced their "marriage,"
contracted outside Jewish Law,
because she was the wife of his brother, Philip.
"Whatever you ask I will give to you,"
Herod said drunkenly to the girl.
She asked her mother, who told her to ask for
the head of John on a platter.
Herod had John killed
and his head was brought to the girl,
who then gave it to her mother.

Prophets clearly denounce injustices of the present,
but when they speak of the future
they generally use rather vague terms.
John used words that both reveal and hide,
words that could be understood
only by those enlightened by the Spirit of God
and rooted in the prophets of the past,
especially Isaiah.
Those prophets announced the one
who would be sent by God,
the Messiah or the Christ,
which means the "anointed one,"
to bring universal peace and the Kingdom of God.

The Jewish people in all their humiliation and despair
were waiting anxiously
for the "one who is to come."
Some thought he would come as a leader of the Zealots

to push the Romans into the sea through violence.
Others thought he would act
through obedience to the Law.
Others were waiting,
not knowing how he would come
but believing that he would be the king of Israel,
a descendant of David,
and would restore the Kingdom.

�֍

To understand Jesus
one has to understand the history of the Jewish people
and their belief that they were the chosen ones of God
who would bring light and salvation to humanity.
Abraham is the father of the Jewish people
and of all believers.
He was led by God away from his land;
then there were Isaac, his son,
and Jacob, his grandson.
Moses was the prophet called by God
to deliver the Jews from slavery in Egypt.
He led them through the Red Sea
towards the promised land.
Moses received the Law from God.
The history of the Jewish people
with their kings, their priests, and their prophets
is the history of a people
frequently crushed and humiliated,
obliged to leave their land,
frequently unfaithful,
yearning to have the power and wealth
of the pagan people,
seduced by idols,
rejecting the prophets sent by God.
Yet always there remained a faithful few
singing their trust in God.

The prophets had announced that
the Messiah,
the Anointed One,
the Christ,
would restore the Kingdom of Israel,
the Kingdom of God,
a Kingdom of peace and of love.
Isaiah had prophesied that a child
named "Emmanuel," "God-with-us" (Is 7),
would receive on his shoulders
the power of God
and be named

> "Wonderful Counsellor,"
> "Mighty God,"
> "Everlasting Father,"
> "Prince of Peace."

He would reign on the throne of David (Is 9).
The Spirit of the Lord would rest upon him;
he would bring an everlasting peace,
where the wolf would live with the lamb
and a child would play near the hole of the cobra (Is 11).
And this servant of the Lord,
the chosen one,
would be gentle,
not shouting out
nor lifting up his voice (Is 42).
His light would shine for all the nations.
All of humanity would follow this chosen one.
Peace would reign over the earth.

> "Arise and shine, for your light has come
> and the glory of the Lord rises upon you.
> Nations will come to your light
> and kings to the brightness of your dawn.
> Lift up your eyes and look about you.
> All assemble and come to you." (Is 60)

Some of the more pious of the Jewish people
were waiting for this Messiah
whose light would shine on all nations
and bring all nations to peace.
Swords then would be beaten into ploughshares
and spears into pruning hooks (Is 2).

John, inspired by the Holy Spirit,
gave Jesus three names:

> "Lamb of God
> who takes away the sins of the world,"
> "Bridegroom,"
> "Son of God, the chosen one, the unique one."

What meaning could these strange names have
for those who listened to the prophet?

For the Jewish people,
many of whom were shepherds and land owners,
the lamb was of particular significance.
They sacrificed lambs in the Temple,
worshipping the Lord through this offering
and proclaiming their obedience to God.

But the lamb has a deeper significance.
Moses was sent by the Lord
to liberate the Jewish people from slavery;
he warned their Egyptian masters
that if they did not obey the Lord and let his people go,
all the firstborn in their families would die.
He told his Jewish brothers to put the blood of a lamb
on the doorpost of their houses
and this would protect them.
So it was that the firstborn of Jewish families
were spared,
and Moses led the Jewish people across the Red Sea
to freedom.

Each year the Jewish people are called to remember
and to celebrate this event
on the feast day they called the "Passover"
because the exterminating angel of the Lord
had passed over their houses,
which had the blood of the lamb on their doorpost.
They ate the paschal lamb,
celebrating the power of God
who had chosen them
and saved them
and led them to freedom.
The lamb of God is the paschal lamb
sacrificed and eaten.

The lamb of God is also
the suffering servant
announced by the prophet Isaiah (53):
led to the slaughter
he opened not his mouth,
yet it is through his wounds
that all are healed.

✄

The "Bridegroom" too had a deep meaning
for the Jewish culture.
Marriages were celebrated with great festivity.
Family and race were important.
The prophets had used this reality of love and union
to reveal the love and union of God
with the chosen people of God.
The Lord is the Bridegroom;
the people are the beloved, the bride, of God.
Ezekiel, Hosea, Jeremiah, Isaiah all speak
of this mysterious relationship of God
with the chosen people:
the relationship of a Lover with the beloved;
God rejoicing over the beloved;

God rendering the beloved beautiful,
crowning her in love,
forgiving her
and calling her back,
when she had fallen into harlotry and infidelity.

> "I shall betroth you to myself forever,
> I shall betroth you in uprightness and justice,
> and faithful love and tenderness.
> Yes, I shall betroth you to myself in loyalty
> and you shall know the Lord." (Hos 2)

The inspired Song of Solomon, the song of love,
which sings the yearnings and union
of the bride and the bridegroom,
has been for the Jewish people,
and for all Christian mystics,
the sign of the love of God.
In it the beloved says:

> "Arise my love, my fair one,
> and come away;
> for lo, the winter is past
> and the rain is over and gone.
> The flowers appear on the earth
> and the time of singing has come.

> "O my dove in the clefts of the rock
> in the covert of the cliff
> let me see your face
> let me hear your voice." (Song of Sol 2)

John gives this messianic name to Jesus:

> "I am not the Christ,
> but before him I am sent.
> The *bridegroom* is the one who has the bride,
> but the friend of the *bridegroom*
> who is waiting and who hears him
> rejoices at the sound of his voice.

> This is my joy
> and it is full.
> He must increase
> and I decrease." (Jn 3)

Jesus the Lover,
Jesus the Beloved,
Jesus the Bridegroom
comes to fulfill all the prophecies.
Yes, the Kingdom of God is now at hand.

�

John had heard the voice
resounding from heaven:

> "This is my Son, the Beloved,
> in whom I have put all my joy." (Jn 1)

So he could testify
that Jesus was the *Chosen One* of God.

The elder son, the unique son,
was also important in the Jewish culture:
he is the beloved one.

The prophecy of Isaiah is again fulfilled:

> "Here is my servant whom I uphold,
> *my chosen one* in whom I have pleasure.
> I have sent my spirit upon him,
> he will bring fair judgment to the nations.
> He does not cry out or raise his voice,
> his voice is not heard in the street;
> he does not break the crushed reed
> or snuff the faltering wick.
> Faithfully he presents fair judgment;
> he will not grow faint,
> he will not be crushed
> until he has established fair judgment on the earth,
> and the coasts and islands are waiting
> for his instruction. . . .

"I have made you a covenant of the people
and light to the nations,
to open the eyes of the blind,
to free captives from prison,
and those who live in darkness from the dungeon.
I am Yahweh, that is my name!
I shall not yield my glory to another,
nor my honor to idols.
See how the former predictions have come true.
Fresh things I now reveal;
before they appear I tell you of them." (Is 42)

Jesus was so humble,
so hidden,
that it was necessary that there be a prophet
who prepared the way for him
and indicated clearly
that he was the "one who is to come."

Jesus, Where Do You Come From?

Who is this Jesus,
the Lamb and the Bridegroom,
the Beloved Son and the Chosen One?
Where does he appear from?
Those listening to John
must have wondered about this man,
kneeling humbly in the Jordan
in front of John.

This man did not walk or strut about
like a general or a politician
seeking votes.
He was gentle and walked humbly;
his whole being spoke of lowliness.
Yet in him was the beauty and the youthfulness
of the bridegroom (he was barely thirty years old),
the joyfulness of the lover,

the seriousness too of the one seeking the bride
with a wounded heart.
He had the strength and the certitude
of one who is sent,
knowing he is the Chosen One,
the Beloved of God.

We know little of his early life,
only that he was born in Bethlehem,
conceived through the power of the Spirit
in the womb of Mary (Lk 1),
a young woman of Nazareth.
She was full of grace and of beauty,
full of the Holy Spirit,
hidden woman,
silent woman,
yearning woman,
in love with God and with the Word of God,
truly one of the *anawim*,
the poor of Adonai.
She thirsted for the Kingdom,
weeping at the humiliations of her people,
the chosen people of God,
and at the mediocrity and infidelity of so many.
She thirsted for justice
and for the loving face of God.
It was to her that an angel, Gabriel, was sent
to announce that God had chosen her
to become the mother of the Messiah.
In her love and littleness and yearning she accepted:

> "Behold I am the handmaid of the Lord.
> Let it be done to me according to your word."

And so the Word became flesh
in her fresh and silent womb.
She rejoiced in the love
that conceived her child,

her body, heart, and spirit in silent ecstasy
in the kiss of God.

After this event,
so amazing and great,
yet so little, humble, and hidden
— God becoming flesh —
Mary went in haste to her cousin, Elizabeth (Lk 1),
who had conceived a child,
miraculously, in her old age.
Mary went to be present to her,
to give her support
for Elizabeth had been looked down upon
because of her barrenness
(the value of a woman at that time
was in her maternity,
serving thus the Jewish race).
Now in her old age, she was bearing a child!
Many must have laughed at her,
seeing this as rather comical.
Mary came to be with her.

When these two pregnant women met,
pregnant too with hidden hope,
and Mary greeted Elizabeth,
the child in Elizabeth's womb, John,
who later baptized in the Jordan,
quivered with joy.
Inspired by the Holy Spirit,
Elizabeth cried out:

> "Blessed are you among women
> and blessed is the fruit of your womb!
> How is it that the mother of my Lord comes to me?
> Blessed is she who believed
> that what was told to her by the Lord
> will be accomplished."

Then Mary sang her song,
the song of the Good News,
the song of all those who believe in the love of God
and the God of love:
the song of the poor and the lowly:

> "My soul magnifies the Lord
> and my spirit rejoices in God, my Savior,
> for he has regarded the lowliness of his servant,
> and behold all generations will call me blessed.
> For he who is mighty
> has done great things for me
> and holy is his name.
> His loving kindness is in those
> who hold him in awe
> from generation to generation.
> He has shown strength with his arm;
> he has scattered the proud
> in the imagination of their hearts;
> he has put down the mighty from their thrones
> and brought up the lowly.
> He has filled the hungry with good things
> and the rich, he has sent away empty.
> He has come to the help of his servant, Israel,
> in remembrance of his mercy
> as he spoke to our fathers,
> to Abraham and to his posterity forever."

Mary was married to a man called Joseph,
a just and loving man.
No man has ever loved as he loved Mary.
The beauty of her heart, her spirit,
given, consecrated to God,
radiated the fullness of the Holy Spirit
living within her,
shining through her eyes, her words, her body.
Her being was whole and holy.

Her body, a temple of the living God,
even more so when the Word became flesh within her.

Joseph could not doubt the grace within her
nor her fidelity
when she conceived.
Mary had possibly told him
about the message of Gabriel and the child.

Joseph knew that this grace
was a gift and a mystery
of which he had had no part.
All had been accomplished without him.
Jesus was not his child.
That is why in anguish he resolved to separate himself
from the woman he loved (Mt 1)
and who brought him close
to light and to God.
There was terrible anguish in Joseph's broken heart.
And there was too the humility of the Word made flesh
conceived in a situation that seemed one of shame
and of pain.

In a dream, however,
an angel revealed to him
that he was part of this mystery
and that he should take Mary as his spouse
and name the child conceived by the Holy Spirit of God
"Jesus."
Mary, the beloved one, and the child of the Most High
were then given to him.
In tears of joy he must have rushed to Mary!
As Joseph embraced his beloved,
he also encompassed the child
hidden in her womb.

Joseph was present at the birth
and witnessed the joy and excitement of the shepherds;
he was present when the wise men from the Orient

came to adore the little king (Mt 2);
he brought the child to the Temple (Lk 2)
and heard Simeon's prophecy.
He took his beloved Mary and child
in the middle of the night
as refugees to Egypt
to flee the awful wrath and cruelty of Herod
who killed with the sword
all the babies in and near Bethlehem.
And then in Egypt, as poor refugees,
he must have heard the child call him "abba,"
"daddy," "beloved little father."

When Herod, the one called the Great, died,
this little family settled in Nazareth,
a poor and despised village
of Galilee.
They lived poorly among the poor.

For some twenty-eight years
Jesus lived there
hidden among the powerless, the weak,
and the lowly ones,
the son of a carpenter.
For twenty-eight years he lived the beatitudes
before announcing them,
fulfilling his humanity,
living humbly,
rejoicing in creation,
humiliated by the Romans,
but loved by God, his Father,
poor,
but filled with the richness of love and of faith
in communion with Mary, his mother,
and with Joseph.

How he, the Word made flesh,
lived, prayed, worked, created, celebrated

with Joseph and with Mary
remains a secret
to be revealed in the final wedding feast.
But throughout her life,
Mary kept all these things in her heart.
How he lived the unity of the Trinity
in the unity of the holy family,
how he lived in communion, holy communion,
with his mother
remains hidden, veiled in mystery.
So too how he lived with the poor,
the weak, and the powerless,
identified with them,
eating at the same table with them,
in communion with them.
These years in Nazareth
reveal how he values humanity
and the ordinary life of every human being in family,
especially the poor, the weak, and the lowly.
The Word became flesh
and lived among us
simply and poorly
as a human being
loved by God.

The Gospels reveal the discrepancy between
the silent, hidden presence of God
in the womb of Mary,
in the poverty, the lowly and humble life of Nazareth,
and the seat of power in Jerusalem,
the palaces of Herod and of Pilate.
At one moment Jesus goes forth
to bridge the gap.

II

JESUS _____

Jesus the Man of Compassion

After his baptism by John
and forty days spent in seclusion and fasting
in the desert,
probably close to Jericho,
where he was tempted by Satan,
Jesus returned to Nazareth.
There in the synagogue of his own village
he solemnly read out a passage from the book of Isaiah:

> "The Spirit of the Lord is upon me;
> He anointed me
> to announce good news to the poor
> freedom to captives
> sight to the blind
> liberty to the oppressed." (Lk 4 and Is 61)

Then he proclaimed to all in the synagogue:

> "This day,
> this prophecy is fulfilled"

Here he announces his vision, his program.

The Spirit of the Lord is sending him
not first to the scribes and the Pharisees,
nor to the wealthy and the ruling class,
nor to the seats of power and of learning,

but to the lowly, the sick, and the poor,
the oppressed and the suffering,
to all those who have no voice,
to all those who cannot fulfill the Law
and feel lost,
to all those excluded from the Temple of Jerusalem,
to all those who are seemingly excluded from God,
to all those who are disgraced and in anguish,
to all those who feel caught up in prisons of guilt.

He will reveal to them good news:
not to be afraid
for God is close to them;
God is a forgiving and understanding God
who loves them.
They are of value.
They are precious.
That is the *good news:*
they are the beloved of God,
the chosen ones of God.
There is hope!

Jesus fulfills this prophecy
as he enters into those places
that are forbidden by Jewish Law.
He eats with sinners and tax collectors;
he touches and heals lepers,
proclaiming that those who are impure
in the eyes of the Law
may be pure
in the eyes of God.
He enters into close, healing relationships
with people in pain
and with women.

Unlike John, who baptized in the Jordan,
where the crowds came to him,
Jesus goes out to look for

the unclean ones, the rejected ones,
like a shepherd seeking lost sheep.
He reveals to them that they are truly important;
many are healed,
many find new confidence in themselves.

The Gospels tell of Jesus moved by compassion;
the Greek word *splanchna* implies a physical component.
It is a deep emotion that makes one's stomach turn over.
Jesus is physically and emotionally moved by suffering;
his heart obviously bleeds in the presence of poor people,
rejected, abandoned, and crushed,
who trust in God,
but are like sheep without shepherds.
He suffers with all those who are in pain,
no matter what class, religious group, or nationality
they may be.
There is something in him that cannot stand hypocrisy
and downright injustice
to the lowly, to the crippled, to sick people in need,
crippled too in their hearts, filled with guilt and shame,
crushed by those who were seen as representing God,
the priests, the high priest,
closed up in their wealth and power.
Splanchna can also mean anger.
Jesus is angry with the way the lowly are treated.

In all the chaos of division, hatred,
fear, and anger in Israel
Jesus appears throughout the land
as a man of compassion,
a man of goodness and of kindness
to all those caught up in the pangs of poverty
and the contradictions of life.

Jesus is a man of relationship and of communion,
seeking personal contacts,
touching people, holding hands,

calling each person to trust and to faith,
looking at each one,
loving each one,
in all their pain and poverty,
revealing also to them their beauty
and that they are beloved of God.

✼

Jesus is moved with compassion at the sight of a leper,
excluded and rejected by everyone:
lepers had to ring a little bell
to warn people of their approach;
nobody would come near them
for fear of contagion
and of being branded impure.
The leper cried out to Jesus:
"If you want, you can make me clean" (Mk 1).
Jesus reached out and touched him
as a sign of welcome and recognition of his personhood;
he healed his sickness
but even more his broken heart and broken self-image.

Jesus brought back to life
the twelve-year-old daughter of Jairus,
the leader of the synagogue
who came begging for a cure for his little girl.
Jesus took Peter, James, and John
with him into the house.
However it was too late;
the little girl was already dead.
Jesus went into her room
with her parents and the three disciples:

>   Taking her by the hand he said:
>
>   "Talitha cum," which means,
>   "Little girl, I say to you rise."
>
>   And immediately the little girl got up
>   and walked. (Mk 5)

Such gentleness and tenderness in this scene!
Such love for the little girl and for her parents!

Jesus healed the woman who had had a flow of blood
for twelve years
and had suffered much from many physicians.
With deep faith, she touched Jesus' clothes as he passed.
She was immediately healed!
Jesus felt a power had gone out of him.
He said to the woman:

>"Daughter, your faith has made you well.
>Go in peace and be healed of your disease." (Mk 5)

He did not say "I have healed you,"
but *"your* faith has made you well."
What gentle humility!

Jesus healed the servant of a Roman centurion
(one of the enemies, a pagan!).
He marveled at the faith and trust
this officer had in him:

>"Truly I say to you
>not even in Israel have I found such faith." (Lk 7)

So too with the Canaanite woman of Greek origin
whose daughter was possessed by an evil spirit.
It seemed as if Jesus did not hear her cry.
The disciples sought to send her away.
She persisted.
Jesus feigned not to want to do anything for her,
saying that he had come for the children of Israel
and that "it is not fair to take the children's bread
and throw it to the dogs."
The woman replied:

>"Yes, Lord, yet even the dogs eat the crumbs
>that fall from their master's table."
>Jesus marveled:
>"O woman, great is your faith.
>Be it done to you as you desire." (Mt 15)

The Gospels are filled
with highly descriptive, even colorful,
individual healings,
liberation from evil spirits.
So it was that crowds of people,
all those who were sick and crippled,
came to Jesus
to be healed,
to receive from him
a force that would make them whole.

Jesus was incredibly sensitive,
marvelously human.
He wept.
He wept with Mary when Lazarus died.
He wept over Jerusalem (Lk 19)
because his people had refused to listen
to his message of peace:
the city would be destroyed and many massacred.

Jesus is close to those in anguish.
He came to comfort those living in pain and despair,
unduly weighed down by the prescriptions of the Law:

> "Come to me all you who labor
> and are heavy burdened
> and I will give you rest.
> Take my yoke upon you
> and learn from me,
> for I am gentle and humble of heart,
> and you will find rest for your souls.
> For my yoke is easy to bear
> and my load is light." (Mt 11)

He cries out in the Temple:

> "Let anyone who thirsts
> come to me
> and drink." (Jn 7)

The bleeding heart of Jesus is open
to all those who are lost
in anguish, in guilt,
thirsty for life, for love, for acceptance.
He comes to heal, to save, to free from bondage,
to give rest, to empower
so that each one in faith
may stand up and see and hear
and work for the things of love.

✖

Jesus tells a story (Lk 10)
to reveal who our neighbor is,
the story of a man going from Jerusalem to Jericho,
beaten up by robbers
and left lying half dead on the road.
A priest approaches, sees the man, but passes by.
So too a Levite, one of the priestly tribe.
Then a stranger, a Samaritan, approaches,
sees the man half dead, stops, touches him,
takes him in his arms, and cares for him.
Jesus asks:

> "Who of the three
> treats this man as his neighbor?"

Clearly the third one,
a man of compassion,
moved by the pain and the suffering
of a fellow human being.
Yet he was a Samaritan,
and Samaritans were looked down upon by the Jews,
regarded as heretics,
people who had turned away from the true Jewish religion
and thus were cut off
from the living tree of the chosen people.
They were pushed aside
and looked down on.

Jesus is sensitive to them in their pain
as he is sensitive to women.

Jewish society was very masculine.
Women had the important role of child-bearing,
but they had no voice and no place
in culture or society.
They were often put aside,
seen as inferior.
In the case of adultery,
it was they who were stoned to death,
and not the man,
as if they were necessarily the ones to blame.
Jesus was particularly sensitive to them
and to their pain,
as we shall see.

⌘

The compassion of Jesus
is the compassion of forgiveness.
Many people were locked up in guilt,
feelings of unworthiness,
broken hearts and spirits,
fearful of God, and of being chastised,
rejected by the so-called pure ones,
representatives of God and the Law.
Jesus came to reveal the forgiving face of God,
a God yearning to reveal love and communion,
not a God who condemns and punishes
disobedience to the Law.

⌘

To forgive is to call back
and to reveal that the person is loved, cherished,
and full of worth;
to forgive is to liberate
from the broken, crushed self-image,

from feelings of guilt.
Forgiveness is to refind
the kiss of peace,
the kiss of the covenant,
and then to celebrate unity.

Forgiveness implies an understanding
of our own poverty, wretchedness, brokenness, and sin;
it implies too an openness
to receive the hand and words of love.

The Pharisees and scribes were angered and annoyed
by Jesus' words on forgiveness;
Jesus did not seem to accept all the ritual purifications
of the Law.
He seemed to put himself above the Law.

One day they caught a woman in the act of adultery.
Like angry wolves
wanting to trap their prey
they seized her, half naked,
and dragged her in front of Jesus,
who was teaching in the Temple.

> "Moses says in the Law that a woman like this
> caught in adultery
> should be stoned.
> What do you say?" (Jn 8)

These angry, cruel, hard, law-ridden men
know now that they have trapped Jesus.
If he speaks of forgiveness,
he will be discredited,
revealing that he is not a real disciple of Moses;
if he accepts the stoning of the woman,
again he will be discredited.
"Now we have him!"
Behind their flowing robes, darkened beards,
proud faces, hardened hearts,

they hide and reveal
the self-righteousness of their power and logic.

Jesus says nothing
but bends down and writes in the sand.
"What do you say?" they scream.

Jesus stands up and says firmly:
> "Let him who is without sin
> throw the first stone."

The men, confounded, start slinking off
like angry, beaten, guilty dogs.

Then Jesus looks at the woman;
her shame and fear of death
are transformed into bewilderment.
Who is this man? a prophet?
He looks at her gently, with love,
his voice transformed:
> "Woman, where are they?
> Has anyone condemned you?"

"No," she answers.
> "Neither do I.
> Go and sin no more."

The compassion, forgiveness of Jesus
gives life.
She leaves,
transformed in love,
no longer captive,
chained by guilt,
but freed
to love in faithfulness.

✄

Jesus tells a parable about a young lad (Lk 15),
the youngest of the family,
who asked his father for his share of the inheritance.

The father gave it to him,
and the son went off and spent it all
on women and loose living.
A famine falls upon the land;
the lad is reduced to misery
and has to find dirty jobs,
feeding pigs just to survive.
Broken and ashamed, he thinks of his father
and dreams of returning to him,
not as son, but as servant,
asking for forgiveness.
Disheveled and dirty,
emaciated and hungry,
he returns home.
While he is still a long way off,
the father sees him and, moved with compassion,
runs to meet him,
flinging his arms around him,
and kisses him.
Yes, all along the father has been waiting for him
and welcomes him with such love.
The lad weeps in confusion.
He cannot understand how he can be loved like that.
The father calls the servants:

> "Bring robes, rings, and sandals;
> kill the fattened calf.
> Let us celebrate,
> for my son who was dead
> is alive!"

The men and women listening to this parable,
squandering their money on loose living,
knowing that they squander
their love, their energies, the gift of God,
and the inheritance of their faith even more,
feel discouraged and guilty.
They are moved to tears.

They realize that Jesus has come,
not for the so-called just,
but precisely for them,
for sinners,
broken men and women.
Hope is reborn in them;
they discover that they are not cut off from God:
the Father is there,
waiting for them to return,
and to take them in his arms
and to embrace them lengthily.

Jesus continues the story.
He tells of the elder son who comes in from the fields
and hears the music and the singing of the celebration.
"What is this all about?" he inquires.
The servants tell him of the return of his younger brother
and his father's gesture of love.
Furious, the elder son rushes over to the father,
complaining bitterly:

> "I have been with you all my life,
> and you have never done anything like this for me!
> And this good-for-nothing son comes back
> having lived with prostitutes,
> and you kill the fatted calf for him!"

The elder son may well have been virtuous
and lived according to the laws of morality,
but he did not have a heart
of compassion and forgiveness.
Throughout the ages there have always been
elder sons
who are apparently pure and virtuous
but who are hard of heart,
and younger sons
weaker and more vulnerable,
but more open to forgiveness
and to the call of communion.

Throughout his life and teaching
Jesus reveals a new and deeper meaning of sin.
It is not just disobedience to a written law,
the refusal or incapacity to obey
because of the power of passion or pride.
Sin is the breakage of a relationship of love,
the breakage of a covenant,
the breakage of trust.
It is to say "no" to God and to the vision of love;
it is to turn one's back on Jesus:
"I do not want you and your saving power,
your promises and your love.
I want to do things on my own,
my way."
Sin is to work against love and communion.
It is to put oneself in the place of God,
refusing to submit to truth,
denying reality,
living in lies.
Sin is to destroy life,
to seek death,
to crush the temple of God in people,
to crush the weak and the poor,
to shut oneself off from their cry,
to shut oneself off from one's own deepest cry
and vulnerability;
to refuse one's own gift,
to refuse to believe in self
and in one's own capacity to receive love.

That is why forgiveness
is to take the youngest son in the arms of love
and to embrace him.
And when Jesus says
to the woman taken in adultery:
"Go and sin no more,"
he is also saying:

"Go and never leave me.
Trust that if we are together,
I in you
and you in me,
you are capable of loving
and of giving life to others
in faithfulness."
Jesus came to liberate us all
from the horrible powers of darkness and fear
that block us
and close us up in death.

❦

When a few mothers brought their children to Jesus
to ask him to bless them,
the disciples tried to push these "pestering" women away;
they felt that there were more important things
for him to do,
and anyway he was tired.
Jesus became angry:
"Let these little ones come to me."
He took them in his arms and blest them. (Mk 10)
The heart of Jesus is communion,
a gift of love;
it is thirst for relationship and presence.
His only desire: to abide in love
and in trust
within human hearts.
His heart is broken by the "no"
of people wanting power and independence,
or closed up in depression,
refusing the littleness and ecstasy of communion.

That is why Jesus rejoices
when he meets people who have discovered
the emptiness of power,
of things,

and of flickering distractions,
and who seek communion with him;
he rejoices when he meets little children
who want to be held in love,
when he meets the poor, the weak,
crying out for recognition and for relationship.

In some mysterious way, Jesus is consoled
by the cry of the poor and the broken.
They awaken the cry to give love
hidden in his own heart.
The disciples do not understand Jesus
and his desire to give love;
they are too taken up with their own projects, power,
and the need for messianic and spiritual success.

Jesus is attracted to those who are lonely and rejected
because he too was rejected.
More than anyone else, he understands
the pain of anguish.
He understands the broken-hearted
because his own heart was broken.
Their pain is his pain;
their loneliness is his loneliness;
their cry for love is his cry for love.
No wonder Jesus is attracted to the poor,
the lonely, and the broken.

Jesus is not a rich, generous benefactor,
distributing healing;
he is a lover
crying out to give his secret
of love and communion;
crying out to give himself,
to reveal the love of his Father.
One day, in the Temple, he cried out:

> "Let anyone who thirsts
> come to me to drink." (Jn 7)

He cried out to give love
and is attracted to those who cry out for love.

Jesus Struggles against Lies, Hypocrisy, and Evil

The compassion in the heart of Jesus
is not softness or weakness,
divorced from light and truth.
His compassion implies a real love
and great strength.
For Jesus compassion is also struggle,
harsh struggle,
against the forces of evil, lies, hypocrisy, and prejudice,
which crush the weak,
hurt and devalue people,
preventing them from growing,
in love and dignity.
It is dangerous to confront a system or an institution
embedded in prejudice,
locked in fear,
dominated by lies.

⌘

Jesus does not flee from conflict;
he enters into it,
prepared to confront the powerful,
to stand up to hypocrisy,
to speak with authority,
clearly announcing the truth of God
without compromise
even when it hurts.
Thus, he is pushed aside, criticized, hated.
The leaders want to kill him.
He disturbs many, as we shall see later.
He came unto his own
and his own received him not.
Humanity seems more prepared to live in conflict,

behind barriers and defense mechanisms,
in a world of oppression, fear, and death,
than to change and to receive a new love.
Human beings seem to be
more at ease proving themselves,
fighting with others, living in rivalry and competition
to gain power and admiration.
It is as if there is a powerful world
of darkness and anguish
in each person, in each group,
both a fear of death and an attraction to death
that prevent people from being open to this love.
This is original sin, the fundamental sin,
which seems to cling to our very skin.
That is why gentle, compassionate love
is rejected and misunderstood.
People do not want Jesus.
They do not want to be liberated from darkness.
They do not want the Kingdom of love.
Jesus is whole and holy
as he advances into the darkness of humanity.

His first struggle is with the spirit of evil,
Satan,
who tempts him in the desert with powerful means
to obtain recognition,
to accomplish his mission with ease.
Jesus is clear in his response:

> "Get out of my sight, Satan,
> You shall do homage to the Lord your God
> and worship him alone." (Mt 4)

Jesus listens only to his loving Father
and to the means that God inspires
in weakness and littleness
openness and vulnerability.
Jesus does not seek power,
certainly not political power.

He will not fight to enter the system,
to reform it from within.
He accepts that his road
is to be in communion with people,
and this implies an openness to each one.
But that means that he can be crushed more easily.

During his first pilgrimage to the Holy City,
after his baptism,
Jesus became angry, terribly angry,
at the way the Temple was being defiled
by the presence of money-lenders
demanding huge interests,
and the trade in animals and pigeons (Jn 2).
He made a whip of cord
and drove out the animals,
overturned the money-changers' tables,
scattering their coins,
creating an immense commotion.
"Do not turn my Father's house into a market!"
His heart was burning with zeal and love
for his dishonored Father.

Jesus was confronting the system.
And he continued to do so
as he provoked leaders
by healing on the Sabbath day,
revealing that it is *people* who are important;
laws are for *people*.
God is there for *people*,
for their healing and their growth
in love.
He confronted power,
spiritual power,
power that crushes little people.
If someone scandalizes a little one, Jesus said,
then he or she should be thrown into the sea
with a huge stone around the neck (Lk 17).

If the rich do not share their riches,
then when they die
they will go to the place of torment
and not to the place of peace.
Jesus confronts the rich
and reveals to them the pain and anguish
that will overwhelm them.

Jesus uses his authority
to announce truth.
He cannot accept that the truth be hidden;
he cannot accept compromise;
he cannot accept lies about his Father.
Jesus enters into violent discussion with Jewish leaders
caught up in their desire for power
and closed in on their prejudice.

> "You are from your father, the devil,
> and you prefer to do
> what your father wants.
> He was a murderer from the start;
> he was never grounded in the truth;
> there is no truth in him at all.
> When he lies
> he is speaking true to his nature,
> because he is a liar,
> and the father of lies.
> But it is because I speak the truth
> that you do not believe me." (Jn 8)

He accuses them of closing the Kingdom to people
through all their man-made laws:

> "Woe unto you scribes and Pharisees,
> you hypocrites!
> You shut up the Kingdom of Heaven
> in peoples' faces,
> neither going in yourselves
> nor allowing others to go in who want to." (Mt 23)

His anger towards many Pharisees and scribes is evident:
>"Woe unto you scribes and Pharisees,
>you hypocrites!
>You are like whitewashed tombs
>that look handsome on the outside,
>but inside are full of the bones of the dead
>and every kind of corruption.
>In just the same way,
>from the outside you look upright,
>but you are full of hypocrisy and lawlessness."
>
> (Mt 23)

Yes, Jesus is angry with those who fiddle with the truth
and use the things of God
for their own power and glory.

Jesus' anger is addressed
not just to those who oppose him openly
but also to those of "good will."
When Jesus spoke of his impending death
at the hands of the high priest and scribes,
Peter reacted:
"God forbid, this will never happen to you!"
Implied in these words were:
"Do not exaggerate.
Anyway I will help you."
Peter cannot hear what Jesus is saying;
he cannot accept that Jesus might lose;
he wants to water down Jesus' words.

Jesus reacts powerfully, even violently:
>"Get behind me, Satan!
>You are a scandal to me.
>Your words are words of human beings
>and not of God." (Mt 16)

Jesus is angry and sad
when his disciples do not understand
his loving, compassionate heart,

his call to be close to the weak, to children,
when they do not accept
the demanding message of his love,
the folly of the love of God
and of the God of love,
the total trust he is calling them to.

Jesus Unprotected from Pain

To understand how Jesus lived and acted,
to understand his compassion and anger,
we must understand
that there were no barriers around his heart,
like in us,
barriers that prevent us from being truly compassionate,
barriers that block the flow of love,
barriers that separate us from God
and from reality,
barriers that protect us from pain.

Living with people who have suffered
from rejection and abandonment,
who have felt devalued and useless,
I have begun to understand
how we *all* protect ourselves
from inner anguish, loneliness,
feelings of guilt, worthlessness, and helplessness.
We run away from all the pain of the child within us
by doing things,
creating projects,
seeking distractions
filling the emptiness inside of us.
We try to forget.
We try to prove that we are the best,
the ones who know, an elite,
or else that we are victims of others who are bad.
We put on masks

and pretend to be what we are not,
seeking acclaim and honor.
Or else we fall into deep depression,
maybe even suicidal acts.

Reality and relationships are so often painful.
We are frightened of people
who might hurt or reject us
or try to control us.
We flee this broken world of ours
where there is so much suffering and injustice,
which make us feel guilty.

As children we have all been hurt.
Our first experience of pain
was on that day when, as a little child,
we sensed that we were not wanted by our parents,
when they were angry with us
because we did not fit into their plan
or do what they wanted us to do.
We cried out and disturbed them
when they did not want to be disturbed
or we did something that annoyed them.
We were so little, so vulnerable then,
so in need of love and of understanding.
We could not understand
that this breakage came from the fatigue, emptiness,
inner pain, and wounds of our parents
who could not bear to hear our cry,
and that it was not "our" fault.

We had to escape, then, into dreams, projects, and ideas.
When little children are hurt,
they close themselves up,
hiding behind unexpressed anger, revolt, and grief,
sulking in depression,
or they escape into a world of dreams.
This breakage is like a dagger

entering a fragile heart,
craving for communion.
It causes horrible loneliness, anguish, inner pain,
feelings of guilt and shame.
Children feel they have hurt their parents
and have disappointed them.
No child can understand or bear this inner pain.
Children cannot judge or condemn their parents,
whom they need so much
just to survive.
So they withhold and hide their anger
and blame themselves.
They know then that they are no good,
unloveable,
misfits that nobody wants.

Human beings learn to cut themselves off
from all this inner pain,
and thus from reality,
and especially from the reality of people
who cause or reawaken inner pain.
We are *all* so broken in love, and in our capacity to relate.
We have difficulty understanding others
and wanting their growth and peace of heart.
We can quickly judge or condemn them.
We push them away,
frightened of them.
We hurt each other.
We seek to control or to use others,
or to run away and hide.

Since we were little children we have hidden this pain
deep down within us,
in a forgotten world
with solid barriers around it.
It is in this forgotten world
of early pain, rejection, and confusion
that the thirst for love and communion

is wounded,
and then relationships become dangerous.

So we tend to live not in reality
but in dream, in ideologies, and illusions,
in theories, projects,
things that bring success and acclaim.
The barriers around our hearts are deep and strong,
protecting us from pain.
We live in the past
or in the future
or in a dream.
Our hearts and minds
can gradually become cut off
from our own flesh and emotions,
from the "now" of reality.
We put ourselves at the center of everything.
not nourished by other people
nor by the song of birds
nor by the cry for love
springing from the heart of children,
but by our own selves,
insatiably seeking uniqueness and value
or falling into the snakepits of depression and revolt,
slipping into the "tomorrow" or the "yesterday,"
clutching on to the wounds of the past.

That does not mean that there are no ethics
and morally good or bad actions.
We can choose to do good and to favor life.
But all the brokenness inside us
soils our motivations
as we seek glory and acclaim,
wanting to prove our goodness and value.
We are all in need of deep, inner healing.

And how did Jesus, the Word made flesh,
communicate with flesh,

with people,
with reality?

It is important to understand the inner life of Jesus,
the Word made flesh.

His mother was filled with grace,
filled with the Holy Spirit.
She loved her child as no other mother has loved,
not from a place of emptiness,
holding on to the child,
controlling and possessing the child's freedom
to calm her own inner pain and anguish.
Mary loved from a place of fullness,
giving life,
giving her life
in love.
In Jesus God was fully present,
right from the moment of his conception
because he was filled with grace;
his flesh was imbued with his divinity.
There were, then, no barriers in Jesus,
no system of defense,
protecting him from pain,
no hidden, forgotten, inner world,
no blind spots or shadow areas,
nothing preventing him
from living, speaking, and acting
from the source of his own life,
from his center,
the place of communion;
no need to flee from reality or people
into anger, dream, or ideology,
seeking success and affirmation.
In him there was no fear of people,
no flight into tomorrow or yesterday,
just presence, total presence
to the "now" of today,

the "now" of reality,
the "now" of people,
the "now" of love,
lived in every situation, with every person he met.
He understood as no other
the fears, darkness, and motivations
that govern people and groups,
for he was not blocked by fear or sin.

He knew when and how to act
to produce the desired result
of love, of communion, and of growth in people.
However, as no other holy person
in the history of humanity,
he was totally abandoned,
like a little child and a lover,
in the hands of the Father,
not seeking self,
his own preordained plan,
nor governed by abstract law and theory;
he listened to the gentle, quiet urgings of the Father
in the here and now of life.
For Jesus, God was not absent
from the movement of society and of matter
but rather present in and through them.
Jesus listened to the Father as he listened to his own heart
and as he listened to events and to people,
sometimes in wonder, sometimes in sadness.
He lived each period of his life
as his consciousness emerged
in wonder and in trust,
in constant thanksgiving and discovery.
He could always be like a little child
for there was no breakage in love,
no inner divisions, no need to prove himself.

It is in this total communion with reality
that Jesus loved his Father,

lived in communion with him,
singing trust and adoration.
It is in this communion of love
that the divine and the human intermingled in him,
the eternal word of love flowing through his finite flesh.

Freed from inner barriers,
unprotected from pain,
Jesus was more totally vulnerable to people,
a gentle lover
in love with each person.
From his eyes, his hands, his flesh,
his whole being
flowed this total presence to people
in their uniqueness.
Totally present to each person,
he received more fully the pain of each one.
He took that pain in him;
he suffered with each one;
he touched the deepest need in each one:
the cry for love, for value, for uniqueness,
for intimacy and for communion,
the cry to be.
But he also touched the fears,
the terrible fears of love in each person,
the pride, the need for independence,
the barriers that protect vulnerability
the screams of "no,"
"I do not want you!"
One senses the broken heart of Jesus
when he says:

> "You refuse to come to me
> to receive life." (Jn 5)

The heart of Jesus was so vulnerable;
it suffered more totally as he was pushed away by people.
The love surging up within him,
thirsty to give communion,

to give life,
and to rest in the hearts of people,
is shoved aside.
Gentle, humble lover,
silent lover,
rejected,
in anguish,
the broken heart of a lover.
He experienced pain more deeply than any of us.

Jesus Came to Reveal
the Loving, Gentle Face of the Father

Jesus came to reveal to each and every one of us
the loving, compassionate, forgiving face
of the Father,
of his Father.
So many people are caught up in false notions of God,
a God of anger, a judge,
spying on people,
ready to pounce and to punish,
a God of law
concerned more with rituals and liturgies,
and the sacrifice of animals, ablutions,
what to do or not to do on the Sabbath,
or else a God distant, far off,
not interested in the human condition
and human suffering.

Jesus came to reveal the *true* face of God,
the God of Love,
the God of Truth,
the God of Light,
passionately interested in people
as they are
in their uniqueness,
a God in love with each one

no matter how little or lowly,
attentive to each one
in all his beauty, poverty, and brokenness
in her feelings of shame and weakness,
a God of life
who sees each human life as precious.
Not a God who seeks first of all
to uphold laws and institutions,
so often on the side of the strong, the rich,
and the powerful,
a God who did not come to judge and to condemn
but to save, to heal, to make whole,
to give life and give it to the full.

Again and again Jesus says
that everything he says and does
is from the Father:
he himself proceeds and comes forth from the Father;
he and the Father work continually
one with the other;
he is sent by the Father;
he is for the Father;
he is the beloved Son;
he is in the Father and the Father is in him;
he is one with the Father.
The disciples are drawn to him
by the Father;
it is the Father who reveals to them
that he is the Messiah, the Son of God.

> "In all truth I tell you
> by himself the Son can do nothing;
> he can only do what he sees the Father doing;
> and whatever the Father does the Son does too.
> For the Father loves the Son
> and shows him everything he himself does,
> and he will show him
> even greater things than these,

works that will astonish you.
Thus, as the Father raises the dead
and gives them life,
so the Son gives life to anyone he chooses,
for the Father judges no one;
he has entrusted all judgment to the Son,
so that all may honor the Son
as they honor the Father.
Whoever refuses honor to the Son,
refuses honor to the Father who sent him." (Jn 5)

At the age of twelve
Jesus was becoming more totally conscious
of the call and love of the Father,
more fully conscious of his mission of love.
He had stayed in Jerusalem
while his parents,
thinking he was with the caravan,
started on the road to Galilee
after their pilgrimage to the Holy City.
When Mary and Joseph discovered his absence,
they returned to Jerusalem
looking frantically for him.
On the third day they found him
in the Temple.
Seeing him, they were filled with emotion.
His mother said:

"My child, why did you do that to us?
Look, your father and I,
we have been looking for you in anguish."
He answered: "Why were you looking for me?
Did you not know
that I should be in the house of my Father?" (Lk 2)

The disciples yearn to know the Father
of whom Jesus speaks so much:

"Show us the Father,"
asks Philip,

"that is all we need."
"Do you not understand yet,"
Jesus answers,
"those who see me,
see the Father?" (Jn 14)

The face of the Son
is the face of God:
his hands, his body, his words, his heart
are those of God,
those of the Father.
The Word became flesh
to reveal the Father.

As no prophet has done in the past
Jesus calls God
"my Father,"
even more, "Abba," "Daddy," "Dad," "Papa."
He is clearly in love with the Father
and the Father in love with him.
There is a deep intimacy between the two,
a communion,
a gift of one to the other,
eternally together,
one in another,
one for the other,
totally equal one to another.

Jesus is totally in communication and in communion
with the Father, with God;
more totally than any mystic or any prophet
or any man or woman of God
in the whole of history.
There are no barriers around his human heart
protecting him from pain and hurtful relationships
preventing too this total communion with God,
this flow of love.
Jesus is totally one with God,

given to God,
receiving all from God,
inspired at every instant by God,
totally surrendered to God,
totally empowered by God,
filled with divine strength and divine littleness.

The Pharisees cannot stand
the affirmation of the unity between Jesus and the Father:
"Being a man he makes himself God" (Jn 10).
This is the ultimate blasphemy
or rather the ultimate mercy and revelation:
the face of God revealed
in the gentle, loving, compassionate face of Jesus,
inviting each person into communion
and a covenant of love.

❀

Here we see how our human words and language
are so limited
as is the reality from which the words come
and which is signified by them.
God is neither male nor female
but clearly transcends both.
We human beings are so pragmatic.
Words flow from our experience of reality.
We have difficulty in touching the truth of words.
We are so locked in emotion and pain.
God is not a father
like our limited, broken, fearful fathers.
In fact our own fathers can be the very opposite
of God the Father.
So for some, calling God "Father"
is painful,
unless they are able to sense
that their very anger in respect to their own father
is a sign that in some way they understand

what true fatherhood is,
thus who is the Father in heaven.

The Father of Jesus is the source.
The Son proceeds from the Father
but is not born once and for all
as we are;
he is eternally being born
in the eternal "now,"
proceeding from the Father,
flowing from the Father.
That is why we have to purify our concept of fatherhood
in order to apply it to God.
For us, a human father precedes the son in time
and normally dies before him;
he is there to educate and guide
his son's life.
Not so for the Trinity.
The Father does not precede in time
nor does the Father educate the Son to leave him.
The Father is the origin
but also the end;
the Son proceeds eternally from the Father
and finds his being,
his personhood,
in the total and absolute gift of his being to the Father.
In our human reality
it is the mother who bears the child in her womb;
the child flows and proceeds from her.
In the Trinity, Fatherhood is also Motherhood.
In the Blessed Trinity
the Son is all *for* the Father;
his very being is all love and gift
towards the Father,
in glory and light.
Here our human words fail.
As we catch a glimpse of the life of God,

three in one,
the analogy of the father and son
must be completed by others,
the analogy of man and woman,
one in spousal love, in partnership,
in total gift and communion,
one with the other,
in the other,
in the glory of the wedding feast.
Man and women together in communion
are the icon or image of God
revealing the mystery of God (Gen 1).
This analogy, however, remains inadequate,
for man and woman need each other,
are different from and complementary to one another
whereas the three persons of the Trinity
are not different substantially,
do not need each other:
each one is fully God.
The Trinity is not a hierarchy of power
but a communion of love.

The love of the three divine persons
one for the other,
one in the other,
contains all the shades of love and friendship
that exist between human beings:
gentleness, kindness,
burning passion,
total trust,
humility and tenderness,
stillness and resting,
one in another.
It contains also all forms of gift of self to another
and of joy.

At the origin,
before all times,

there is this life and love and light,
this joy, communion, and ecstasy
between the Father and the Son,
the eternal embrace
from which proceeds
the Third Person of the Trinity,
the Holy Spirit,
totally equal to the Father and to the Son,
totally one with them.

And Jesus,
in communion with the Father,
teaches his disciples to pray,
to enter into that same communion
that he lives with the Father.
He teaches them to say simply:

> "Our Father,
> who art in heaven,
> hallowed be thy name;
> thy Kingdom come,
> thy will be done
> on earth as it is in heaven.
> Give us this day our daily bread.
> Forgive us our trespasses
> as we forgive those who trespass against us.
> Lead us not into temptation,
> but deliver us from the Evil One." (Mt 6)

And he tells them to ask continually
and they will receive.

> "Can you imagine," he says,
> "a child asking for an egg
> and the father giving him a scorpion?
> So, too, will your Father in heaven
> give his Holy Spirit
> to all who ask." (Lk 11)

> "Whatsoever you ask the Father,
> in my name,
> you will receive." (Jn 15)

Jesus reveals to his disciples
how they are loved by the Father;
how he wishes to answer
their deepest cry and deepest call
and to lead them into the ecstasy of life,
into eternal life.

Jesus comes to reveal
that God is a humble God of Love
who offers a relationship of love and of communion
to each person,
not imposing, not obliging,
but inviting: "come,"
waiting too
for each one to unlock the doors of pride and independence
and the need to prove oneself
and to say to God
"come."

The "come" of God,
the "come" of the creature,
is the embrace of God and humanity.
Yes, we humans are called to enter into
the glory and the ecstasy of the life of God.
Jesus calls his disciples into this union of love.
In communion with Jesus,
we enter into the very life of God.
Jesus calls and invites
to trust,
to belief,
to enter into communion with him.
He reveals to his followers:

> "As the Father loves me,
> I love you."

And he prays an incredible prayer to the Father:

> "that the love with which you have loved me
> may be in them,
> and I in them." (Jn 17)

This is the ultimate revelation:
Jesus loves people; he loves each one.
Jesus loves his disciples
and calls them to be his friends (Jn 15)
not just servants.
He invites each one into the to-and-fro of love,
which constitutes communion and friendship.

Jesus is not a distant, benevolent, just leader,
the great king
who will reorganize humanity
in justice harmony and peace.
After having fed the five thousand
many wanted Jesus to be such a king (Jn 6),
more worthy than Herod,
but that is not what Jesus came to accomplish.
Having escaped from their sight
and traveled across the lake,
he began to announce the secret of his heart:

> "In all truth I tell you,
> if you do not eat the flesh of the Son of man
> and drink his blood,
> you have no life in you.
> Anyone who does eat my flesh
> and drink my blood
> has eternal life,
> and I shall raise that person up on the last day.
> For my flesh is real food
> and my blood is real drink.
> Whoever eats my flesh and drinks my blood
> lives in me
> and I live in that person." (Jn 6)

Jesus did not come to be a great political leader,
but the gentle lover of people,
empowering them to love as he loves.
He came to reveal the intimacy he lives with the Father
and to call us to enter into that intimacy
by entering into intimacy with him.
This intimacy is given and signified
as each one eats his flesh and drinks his blood.

The people wanted a great and powerful leader,
but Jesus came to offer them something else:
love and communion through his flesh,
a mystical union with him.
He came to be the gentle lover,
tending hearts,
calling forth in people
their deepest energies of love,
not first of all in generosity
but in communion,
a communion of love.

When they heard these words
many turned away:

>   "These words are too hard.
>   Who can listen to them?"

They would rather have power,
political or social power,
than the littleness of love.
They would rather be heroes
than gentle, humble lovers.

Yesterday, as today,
it is difficult for people to understand Jesus,
the gentle lover,
clothed in weakness,
offering a new love,
calling people into an ecstasy
of intimacy and glory,

the eternal wedding feast,
which is the very life of God.

Jesus Announces the Kingdom

John the Baptist announced
that the Kingdom of God was near at hand.
Jesus announces that the Kingdom is already here
among us (Lk 17).

The Jewish people were waiting
for the coming of the Kingdom;
the poor, the crippled, the lame, and the blind
the lowly, the weak, and the oppressed,
those who had no voice,
were yearning for the Kingdom.
For years many had felt excluded from the Temple
and the proximity of God.
They were waiting
in trust,
maybe also in anger and in revolt,
not knowing, not seeking to know
how it would come about.

Others were waiting for the Kingdom of Israel
to be restored in an external way,
maybe even through violence,
the victory of God over the pagan oppressors
would be evident.
The name of God,
the holy name of God
would again be revered throughout the land.
The chosen people would rediscover
their dignity and power.

Jesus came to announce something entirely new,
difficult to understand,
not an external Kingdom

with a visible, powerful king
surrounded by competent ministers and rulers,
but a Kingdom visible only to the eyes of the heart
and of faith,
small, like a mustard seed,
invisible, like yeast in the dough (Mt 13),
yet within each there is a secret power:
within the seed is contained
a huge bush or tree that is to come
and the yeast makes the bread rise.

This Kingdom is not for those who are big and mighty,
closed in on their knowledge and power,
but for those who are like children
with the simplicity, trust, and openness
of children (Mt 19),
because it is the Kingdom of Jesus
and Jesus is the child of the Father,
a little one,
who receives all from the Father
and gives all to the Father.

This Kingdom is like a new world.
In order to enter into this city of love,
there must be a transformation,
a rebirth:

> "Truly, truly I say to you,"
> said Jesus to Nicodemus,
> "no one can see the Kingdom of God
> without being born again." (Jn 3)

The Kingdom of God is for the poor, the weak,
the lowly, and the powerless (Mt 5).
It is more difficult for a rich person to enter the Kingdom
than for a camel to pass
through the eye of a needle (Mt 19).
The rich in the biblical sense are
those who are closed in what they possess,

wealth, knowledge, certainty, power, and self-satisfaction
in which they put all their trust and security.
The poor, the poor in spirit,
naked in human security,
put their trust in God.
The Kingdom is where the poor, the lowly, and the children
are honored.
It is they who are at the center,
no longer the mighty of the earth,
the stars and prize winners.
It is they who are called to be filled to overflowing
in the celebration of love
flowing from the Trinity.

The Kingdom is like a treasure
hidden in a field (Mt 13),
in the field of the human heart
and for which one gives up everything.
This treasure brings an inner freedom,
peace and joy unheard of,
that no one can imagine,
something so new, totally new,
that it is worth leaving everything to obtain it.

Yet the Kingdom is a gift,
a gift of God,
not earned through good actions, piety,
or obedience to the Law.
It is given by the Father
to those who yearn for it
who thirst
and cry out humbly,
who trust in Jesus;
it is theirs for the asking
but they must ask for it
like little children
yearning.

"Fear not, little flock,"
says Jesus,
"for it has pleased the Father
to give you the Kingdom." (Lk 12)

The Kingdom of God
hidden in our human flesh
grows gently.
It does not appear totally, instantly.
The Kingdom of God is like a sower
going out to seed (Mt 13);
the seed is the word of the Kingdom;
it grows,
but it must be tended and nourished
so that it can bear much fruit.
It is fragile
and can be quickly stifled by weeds
of seduction and the worries of the world.

The Kingdom of God is like a wedding feast (Mt 22).
It is the wedding feast
of love and of unity,
the ecstasy and joy and celebration
of the Trinity,
where the Son receives all from the Father
and gives all to the Father
in the ecstasy of gift and communion.
The poor and the little come to the wedding feast;
the rich are too busy;
they have no time for it.
Those who come receive all and give all,
replenishing themselves at the Source
or the table of love,
emptying themselves
as they themselves become a source of love.
They drink and give water deeply,
becoming a spring of water for others
in an eternal flow of celebration.

The Kingdom of God is a way of life
announced by Jesus
as a place of blessedness,
a place where God is present.
The Kingdom is for the poor (Mt 5),
those who are poor in spirit,
insecure but trusting,
and who are without anger or despair;
the Kingdom is for the gentle and the non-violent,
not the violent nor the timid, those who flee conflict.
It is for those who weep, yet do not close up,
and for those who are hungry and thirsty
for the things of God,
yet not militant or condemning of others.
It is for those who are merciful,
yet not with condescension, pity, or a sense of superiority.
It is for those who are pure of heart,
without pride,
and for those who are peacemakers,
not seeking to impose their ways.
The Kingdom is for those who, like Jesus,
are put aside and crushed
for Jesus and for the truth
and who remain without bitterness or desire for revenge.
This is the path and the way of the Kingdom.
It is a place of love
where we are reborn,
liberated from the prison that kept us locked in ourselves,
in fear and continual concern for self-glory.
The Kingdom is where we turn the other cheek
when slapped,
walk the extra mile,
give our tunic as well as our coat,
where we no longer judge or condemn others (Lk 6),
but forgive, forgive, and forgive in compassion;
where enemies are loved
and prayed for (Mt 5);

where those who speak evilly
are spoken well of.
It is possible to give and give and give
in this way
only because we are continually receiving.
We can become a source for others
only because we are drinking from the source.
It is possible to let down defense mechanisms
and barriers of protection
only because we know we are protected and held by God.
That is the Kingdom.

Jesus called his followers to look at the birds of the air;
they neither sow nor reap,
yet the heavenly Father gives them all they need.
So too the lilies of the fields:
they are clothed in a way
that surpasses Solomon in all his glory.

> "O you of little faith...
> seek first the things of the Kingdom
> and all the rest will be given to you.
> Do not be anxious about tomorrow.
> You are more precious to the Father
> than the birds of the air." (Mt 6)

Abandon yourself in trust
to the One who loves you.
Little children,
like Jesus,
cry out to the Father,
"Abba, "Daddy."
The Father is looking after you.

Jesus came to draw us all
into the hidden Kingdom
of love.
It is present here and now,
not in palaces

or museums,
but in the hearts of the poor and the lowly,
in those who are like little children
in our own loneliness
and in the child hidden in each one of us.
It is in the unexpected places of suffering and of pain,
in the prisons and the slums,
in the hospitals,
and the untouchables of our times.
It is in all those who are broken, excluded,
those who are cast out,
all those who are naked and crucified today.

The Kingdom of God now hidden
in the places of rejection and brokenness
will one day be revealed
in all its fullness.
The eternal wedding feast
will shine in all its glory
more brilliant than the sun.
It will become the source of light
for the sun will have passed away.

On that day, the King will come
in all his glory
with all the angels;
he will sit on the throne of glory.
All the nations will assemble in front of him
and he will invite into the Kingdom
all those who with compassion
have touched and succored and welcomed
the poor, the broken, the hungry,
the strangers, saying:

>   "Come blessed of my father
>   take in inheritance
>   the Kingdom prepared for you
>   since the foundation of the world." (Mt 25)

Jesus announces a Kingdom hidden in human hearts.
This Kingdom is not present in people
caught up only in law,
wanting only to preserve the values of yesterday,
nor in those only urging change
through external and political power,
caught up in a vision for tomorrow.
Jesus neither imposes law
nor throws it out for change.
He reveals a new law of love,
of compassion,
of forgiveness,
in the "now" of today.
He reveals a new priority:
to be present to the poor and to the weak;
for it is they who will lead people
into the Kingdom;
they are the key to the Kingdom.

And Jesus is the King of the invisible Kingdom,
hidden in the heart of this broken world of ours,
hidden in the broken hearts of the world.
Jesus did not want to be a visible, political king,
exercising an external authority.
He fled when people tried to make him king.
But he affirms to Pilate that he is a king.
He is the silent, secret
King of love,
King of our hearts,
yearning to embrace each one of us
with the gift of inner freedom,
setting us free to love.

The Kingdom of Jesus is not of this world.
It is the Kingdom of the Trinity,
the Kingdom of love.
Jesus will leave this world physically.
He affirms to Peter:

"You are Peter, the rock,
and on this rock I will build my Church
and the powers of death shall not conquer it.
I will give you the keys of the Kingdom
of heaven.
What you forbid on earth
shall be forbidden in heaven
and what you allow on earth
will be allowed in heaven." (Mt 16)

The littleness of Jesus
as he confides an authority
to us poor, broken, human beings.

Jesus Weeps to Bring All into the Kingdom

Jesus weeps
in the face of all the divisions he sees and touches
among his people:
the poor, the weak, the sick, the crippled,
like Lazarus lying in the street,
the oppressed, the so-called sinners,
reduced to loneliness,
the homeless,
unwelcomed,
separated from Jewish society,
and on the other side
the rich, the powerful, the comfortable, the "pure,"
settled in their secure ways.
And Jesus weeps
in the face of all the divisions, hatred, and oppression
between Romans and Jews,
Jews and Samaritans,
the pure and the impure.

The heart of Christ weeps for unity
to draw together into the Kingdom,
into one city of love,

the weak and the strong,
the poor and the comfortable,
the powerless and the powerful,
the Jews and the Gentiles,
that there may be
no more competition and rivalry,
no more hiding behind closed walls of prejudice,
no more racism or sexism,
no more rejection of the weak and the powerless,
no more aggression, wars, manufacture of armaments.
In the vision of Jesus
each one has a place
and is called to love and to exercise his or her gifts
to build the body of community
and to reflect the unity of the Trinity.

The yearning in the heart of Jesus
expressed in his final prayer to the Father
is that

> "they may be one,
> as we are one,
> I in them
> and they in me,
> so that they may be totally one." (Jn 17)

The heart of Christ has a vision for humanity:
humanity not governed or organized as a hierarchy
where the powerful, the wealthy, and the honored
are at the top
and the slaves and the marginalized,
crushed and humiliated
at the bottom,
but humanity born into a body
centered upon the weakest,
where all are bonded together in communion
and where each one,
particularly the weakest,

is honored:
communities of the Kingdom.

That is why Jesus began his ministry
by announcing his program of love,
the "Good News"
to the poor, the oppressed, the captives.
His desire is to reform humanity
into a body of love
and he begins precisely with the poorest,
for they are the foundation stone
of this new and wonderful edifice.

Jesus shares this vision with the disciples.
He calls them not just to be in union with him
and to know the Father,
but to live as he lived,
to share his vision of humanity,
to work so that the Kingdom may become a reality.
This implies not only a change of heart and deep faith,
not just prayer but human wisdom,
inspired by the Spirit of God,
a new way of exercising authority
in communion with one another,
working together in love,
respectful of the call and place of each one,
especially of the weak and the little,
listening to them;
hearing their prophetic voices
calling for change,
respectful also of all those who are different
and in whom the light of God is present
but hidden.

To bring about this Kingdom,
the city of love
Jesus was close to people of all walks of life:

to Jews and Samaritans,
to men and women,
to the pagan woman he healed,
to the servant of the Roman soldier.
He broke through all the boundaries
of country, culture, race, and religion,
meeting and loving *people*.

The message of Jesus is one of universal love:
each person is our brother, our sister;
those who are strange and different,
the Romans and the Samaritans,
are also children of God.
People are no longer to be closed in upon themselves,
behind the barriers that protect them
from pain, from reality, from others,
but they are called to open wide their hearts
to this new vision of humanity,
a vision of unity.

Humanity had closed itself into groups,
surrounded by physical, cultural,
and psychological barriers,
with armies to defend them
or to attack in order to expand
and gain more land and wealth.
Each group had its culture, language, and religion.
Each one considered itself the best
and despised others
or were frightened of them.
The Jewish people were a cohesive group,
like many others,
with rigid laws, a unifying hope, a strong identity
through their belief in God
and in their own sacred history and destiny.
Their race was marked in their flesh.
They knew they were the chosen people.

Jesus came to break down the barriers
that protected groups
and gave them a clear identity.
He came to draw all people into oneness
in and through his flesh.

This new vision of unity for humanity,
lived and announced by Jesus,
disturbed the security and the force
of the Jewish identity and vision;
it endangered the system and the culture
and the way of life of many,
as it has endangered religious groups
throughout history.

Unity is not, however, fusion or conformity.
Every one is different.
Every one is unique.
Every one has a gift to give
for the construction of the Kingdom
and of the body of humanity.
In the human body there are many parts,
different one from another,
but one body:
it is unity in diversity.

But how can we break down these walls
built up around hearts, families, tribes,
groupings of people
in nations and races?
These walls, stronger than concrete,
founded on fear,
protect people from insecurity and anguish.
Without walls they feel they might disappear
into emptiness.

This Kingdom of Love will come about
not through hate and violence,
for "those who use the sword

will perish by the sword" (Mt 26),
but through a rebirth of each person in love,
through the gift of the Holy Spirit,
when light penetrates and transforms darkness.
It will be a transformation and change
of heart and of direction for each one,
through the acceptance of a path
of insecurity
and of humility,
trusting totally in Jesus,
becoming poor,
sharing wealth and power.
It will be through forgiveness and reconciliation,
through a deep and total commitment to the poor,
eating at their table (Lk 14),
rising up in community and in solidarity with them.
It will be through commitment to light and to truth.

Jesus called his disciples to the impossible:

> "Love your enemies;
> do good to those who hate you;
> speak well of those who speak evil of you;
> pray for those who persecute you." (Lk 6)

Yes, this is the impossible love
that Jesus comes to announce
in order that humanity work towards unity.
This way of non-violence, forgiveness, and reconciliation,
of acceptance of people who are different
of total commitment and identification with the poor,
given as a gift of the Holy Spirit,
will shake all the foundations
of societies closed in upon themselves:
dictatorships
or unbridled liberal capitalism.
It will be a new force
given by Jesus
in love

where hate is transformed
into forgiveness
and enemies into friends.
This transformation will take time,
for the Kingdom grows
little by little
like a seed;
it is founded on love and on communion.

However, the resistance to Jesus
and to the Kingdom
is great
in the heart of each one of us.

Who Does Jesus Claim to Be?

John the Baptist attributed to Jesus
the messianic names:
lamb,
bridegroom and lover,
chosen one.
He indicated clearly
that Jesus was
the "one who is to come."

As we have seen, Jesus himself
affirmed that he was the Christ
when he announced that the prophecy of Isaiah (61)
was fulfilled this day:

> "The Spirit of the Lord is upon me.
> He has consecrated me
> to announce good news to the poor." (Lk 4)

In Hebrew as in Greek,
"Christ" means "the consecrated (or anointed) one."
So this text could read:

> "The Spirit of the Lord is upon me.
> He made me Christ
> to announce good news to the poor."

Jesus healed many
though he continually affirmed to them:
"your faith has made you whole."
It is not just the healing power
flowing from his flesh
but also the "faith power"
in the person healed.

When John the Baptist was in prison,
in a moment of doubt and anguish,
he sent his disciples to Jesus to ask:

> "Are you the one who is to come
> or should we wait for another?" (Mt 11)

Jesus said to them:

> "Go and tell John what you hear and see:
> the blind see again,
> the lame walk,
> the lepers are cleansed,
> the deaf hear,
> the dead are raised up
> and the poor hear good news.
> Blessed is the one who is not scandalized by me."

The healings Jesus accomplished were signs
that he was truly the Messiah.
Jesus himself was discreet about his role.
He told many he had healed
to say nothing about him.
He was concerned
that all too quickly people would take him as the Messiah
they aspired to and wanted,
and not as the Messiah he really was,
thus causing disturbances and political upheaval

before the time was ripe,
before his hour had come.

Only once did Jesus affirm directly and clearly
that he was the Messiah,
and that was to the Samaritan woman,
one of the most wounded, humiliated, and despised women
of the Gospels (Jn 4).
And when Peter said to him:

> "You are the Christ,
> the Son of the Living God,"

Jesus answered:

> "Blessed are you Simon Bar Jona.
> For flesh and blood have not revealed this to you
> but my Father who is in Heaven." (Mt 16)

Jesus frequently referred to himself as
"the Son of Man,"
a more discreet messianic title
whose origins one finds in the prophet Ezekiel
and the book of Daniel
where the prophet foresees in a vision
the final struggle between good and evil,
God and Satan:

> "I was gazing into the visions of the night,
> when I saw, coming on the clouds of heaven,
> as it were a Son of Man.
> He came to the One most venerable
> and was led into his presence.
> On him were conferred rule, honor, and kingship,
> and all peoples, nations, and languages
> became his servants." (Dan 7)

It is precisely this prophecy
that Jesus attributes to himself
when, during his trial,
the high priest Caiaphas summons Jesus
to answer the question:

> "I command you in the name of the living God
> to tell us if you are the Christ, the Son of God."

Jesus answered him:

> "It is you who say it.
> But I tell you that from this time onward
> you will see the Son of Man
> seated at the right hand of the Power
> and coming on the clouds of heaven." (Mt 26)

The Jews themselves were conscious that
Jesus was claiming for himself the name of God:
this was the ultimate blasphemy
for which was reserved in Jewish law
condemnation to death (see Lev 24).

When Jesus said to a paralyzed man:

> "Your sins are forgiven,"

the scribes and the Pharisees began to think

> "Who is this person who blasphemes?
> Only God can forgive sins." (Lk 5)

And when Jesus affirmed his oneness with the Father,
they said:

> "It is not because of your good works
> we want to stone you to death,
> but because you blaspheme,
> because being a man
> you make yourself God." (Jn 10)

Just as earlier it is written:

> The Jews sought to kill Jesus
> because not only did he violate the laws
> of the Sabbath
> but he called God his own Father
> thus claiming equality with God. (Jn 5)

Near the end of that special conversation with Jesus
the woman of Samaria said:

"We know that when the Messiah comes
he will announce all things."

Jesus said to her:

"*I am*
who speaks to you." (Jn 4)

He does not say, "I am he,"
or "I am the one who is to come,"
but "*I am.*"
This is the ultimate name of God revealed to Moses
when Moses asked:

"If they ask me what is the name of God
what shall I say?"

God answered Moses:

"I am who am.
You shall say to the children of Israel,
I am has sent me to you." (Ex 3)

This same name of God is revealed
through the prophet Isaiah:

"You are my witnesses," says Yahweh,
"and my chosen servant,
that you may know and believe in me
and understand
that *I am;*
before me no God was made
and after me none shall be.
I am.
I am Yahweh
and except I am
there is no savior.
I am
who has announced and saved and made known
and not a stranger.
Yes, you can testify —
this is the word of God —
I am

> since the origins
> *I am.*" (Is 43)

In the eighth chapter of John
Jesus affirms this name "I am":

> "You are from below
> I am from above;
> you are from this world,
> I am not of this world.
> I told you
> that you would die in your sins;
> for if you believe not
> that *I am*
> you will die in your sins.
> When you lift up the Son of Man
> then you will see that
> *I am.*"

And then later,

> "Truly, truly I say to you
> before Abraham was
> *I am.*" (Jn 8)

And again, during the last meal,

> "I tell you this now
> before it takes place
> that when it does take place
> you may believe that
> *I am.*" (Jn 13)

And Jesus affirms:

> "I am the light of the world.
> I am the way, the truth and the life.
> I am the Good Shepherd
> I am the resurrection.
> I am the Bread of life.
> I am the true Vine,
> without me you can do nothing."

�֍

John the Evangelist affirms the divinity of Jesus
at the very beginning of his Gospel:

> In the origin was the Word
> and the Word was towards God
> and the Word was God.
> He was in the origins
> towards God;
> all things were made through him
> and without him
> not one thing was made.

And then the revelation:

> And the Word became flesh
> and dwelt among us.

This revelation became clear to John
only after the resurrection of Jesus
and after he had been filled with the Holy Spirit.
During his time on earth,
Jesus discreetly affirmed his divinity,
but even those who followed him and loved him
could not hear this.
He was so simple,
so loving,
so like everyone else,
yet different
because more totally loving
and more totally "surprising" in every way.
They had not the power in them
to understand or to believe
that Jesus,
the man they loved and followed,
was the Word made flesh.
Only Mary understood and believed,
she of whom it was said:

"Blessed are you among women
and blessed is the fruit of your womb."

"Yes, blessed is she who believed
in the fulfillment of all
that had been revealed to her
by the Lord." (Lk 2)

III

JESUS ATTRACTS AND DISTURBS _____

Those Who Were Drawn to Jesus

The first people drawn to Jesus
were the poor, the lame, the broken, and the rejected
who had lost all hope and dignity,
all those who had been pushed aside by the establishment
because of their sinfulness,
because they did not follow the Law.
They felt abandoned by God.

Jesus looked at them,
touched them,
loved them, and healed them.
He reawakened hope in them.
With Jesus
they discovered that they were not evil,
not condemned,
but that they were loved by this prophet
and thus by God.
So many of the beggars,
so many men and women possessed by evil spirits,
once healed
just wanted to remain with him.

They trusted him;
they put their faith in him.

Then there were disciples of John the Baptist
who heard him announce Jesus
as "the Lamb of God."
Drawn to the Lamb,
two of them left him
to become Jesus' disciples.
They spent the day with him,
touched by his presence,
enfolded in his light and love.
And then they called others to him (Jn 2).

Little by little, men and women gathered around Jesus.
They were mysteriously drawn to him
by the Father.
Jesus called them to him.
They were touched by his compassion for the poor,
the weak, and the broken;
they were touched by the way
he spoke with authority,
no quibbling, no casuistry:
the simple language of a prophet,
calling people to trust in God.
They saw in him a man of God,
a prophet,
maybe the Christ.

But people were touched not only by what he said
but even more by the way he lived,
by the radiance and the love that flowed from him.
In him there was no hypocrisy,
no double messages.
There was no separation between
what he said and what he lived.
His words flowed from his life,
not just from his head.

He cared not for ideas or for institutions
but for people, individual people.
He continually sought out
those who were in pain.
People came from afar to be healed
of all their infirmities.
In this man there was such compassion,
goodness, kindness,
but he was also demanding.
A truth, a light radiated from him.
He could not stand lies and hypocrisy
and the using of the name of God
in order to obtain wealth and power.

In Cana of Galilee
at a wedding feast of two poor families
he changed an immense amount of water
into incredibly good wine
in order to save these humble people
from humiliation
but also to reveal
that the Kingdom of God is a wedding feast
and that he came to change the water of our lives
into the warmth of wine;
he came to transform our human lives
into something totally new,
the ecstasy of communion in God.

People were drawn to Jesus
from all walks of life
and for multiple reasons.

Many had been waiting for the Messiah,
"the one who was to come"
to restore the Kingdom of Israel,
to renew the hearts of the lost and the broken-hearted,
to bring freedom.
Was Jesus the Messiah?

Others came just to be healed:
their bodies racked with pain,
their hearts with shame,
not understanding, not expecting
that the healing of their bodies would be a call
to a change of heart and of their lives.

Still others were curious to meet a prophet
and to witness a healing.
Some were drawn to Jesus not quite knowing why.
Some came with childlike hearts
in prayerful awe.
Others were cynical;
others weeping and in need,
and Jesus knew what was in the heart of each one.
Some came to him
because he had sought them out,
in the world of prostitution
and of collaboration with the Roman enemy.
He had looked at them with love
and called them.
They had been locked up in guilt,
their lives a mess,
seeking, squandering money like Levi.
They had been excluded from the Temple
and so they thought they were excluded
by God and from God.
Jesus came to them in love.
His love transformed them,
broke down their barriers,
awoke new energies of life and of love within them.
In this meeting with Jesus
they were liberated.
They began to follow him.

Jesus clearly had a special relationship with women.
It is in a private conversation
near Jacob's well

with a Samaritan woman (Jn 4),
one of the poorest, most rejected women of the Gospels,
a woman of ill repute
who had lived with five men,
that Jesus reveals a deep secret:
if she drinks of the water he will give her
these waters will become in her
"a spring of water welling up to eternal life."
Water, life will flow from her!
She will become a source of life for others.
It is only to this woman
that he revealed that he was the Messiah,
the one that was to come,
the one that *is*.
This he told to no one else but her.
He empowered her in a special way.
When the conversation was over
the Samaritan woman rushed to tell
all the men of the town:

> "Come and see a man who told me
> everything I have done!
> Is he not the Christ?"

They went to him,
and they believed that Jesus was the Savior of the world.

He loved Mary of Magdala in a special way,
Mary of the Roman camp;
she seems to have been a victim of prostitution.
Jesus called her to him
and she became his much-beloved disciple.
This same Mary* breaks open
a bottle of precious ointment
and pours it on the feet and head of Jesus

---

*Contrary to certain biblical scholars, but in accord with a long tradition in the Church and with a new group of biblical scholars, I believe Mary of Bethany is the same woman as Mary of Magdala, that is, Mary of the Roman camp. Here is not the place, however, to give reasons for this.

for he had brought back to life her brother Lazarus
after four days in the tomb (Jn 12).

Judas and the disciples were angry
at such a waste of money (Mt 26)
(the precious ointment could have been sold
for the year's salary of a worker).

Was it their concern for the poor
that made them mutter angrily among themselves
or was it not a certain jealousy
because of the privileged relationship and intimacy
she had with Jesus
and from which they were excluded?
Jesus speaks strongly and lovingly in her defense:

> "Why do you annoy this woman?
> She has done something beautiful for me.
> Truly I say to you
> that wherever the good news is proclaimed
> throughout the whole world
> it shall be said what she did
> in memory of her." (Mt 26)

And after the resurrection
the very first person to whom the risen Jesus appears
is this very same Mary.
He tells her to go and announce the good news
to the brothers.
Later, he reproaches these brothers
for not trusting what she had told them (Mk 16).

The Gospel tells us that

> Jesus loved Martha, Mary, and Lazarus. (Jn 11)

It seems he would often slip away
from the men he had chosen,
who often did not understand him,
to rest
and be with them.

The Gospels tell of the women of Galilee
who served Jesus
discreetly and lovingly;
they were continually present to him
right to the very end.

In the Gospel vision,
women have a unique place;
they seem to understand Jesus better.
Is it because the men were caught up in the project
of the Messiah
rather than with Jesus himself?
Is it because they frequently tended to want *to do* things,
to prove themselves and to organize,
and were a bit fearful of communion?
Is it because women are more in contact
with the essential of love
that Jesus called them
and sent them
as intermediaries towards men?

Both the Samaritan woman and Mary of Magdala
were sent
to give courage and to reveal faith to men.
The Word came first to Mary;
he became flesh in her womb
and lived with her a unique relationship in Nazareth
before going forth to others.
Mary too is an intermediary
between God and others.

Among his followers,
Jesus did choose twelve
to be with him,
to be formed and transformed by him,
to be his friends and companions
in a special way.
He named them "apostles,"

which in Greek means "those who are sent."
Just as he had been sent by the Father,
he was sending these twelve men
to announce good news to the poor,
to liberate the oppressed and the prisoners.
These twelve men left all they had
to follow Jesus:
they left their jobs, their wealth, their land,
their families, even their reputation.
Some had probably been laughed at,
scorned, and rebuked
by so-called friends and family
who did not trust this Jesus from Nazareth,
calling him "another one of those false prophets";
"you will see; it will all end badly."

Some of these twelve were fishermen:
Peter and Andrew, James and John;
Matthew was a publican, a tax collector;
Nathanael (or Bartholomew) seems to have been
a bit of an intellectual,
but none of them was trained and formed
in rabbinic studies.
Each one had his own character,
weaknesses and strengths and foibles.
At first they must have quietly followed Jesus
(even though the step to leave all may have been hard).
Little by little they began to realize
the impact Jesus had upon people.
He was becoming well known,
people were flocking to him from all over Israel,
to listen to him,
to be healed by him.
This must have gone to their heads.
They began to think
that they were going to be in his government
when he restored the Kingdom of Israel

They began arguing among themselves:
"Who is the most important?"
Each one wanted the best place.
The mother of two of them, James and John,
intervened and asked Jesus that her two sons
might be seated one on his left and the other on his right
in his Kingdom (Mt 20).
The others were obviously upset by her
and murmured against her.
These men were very human,
like all of us.
Like everyone else in Israel at the time,
they had their own ideas
about who and how the Messiah should be,
what sort of person he would be,
what he should do.
They were excited by spiritual power,
thrilled to know that they had been chosen
to be part of this Kingdom.
In one way, to follow Jesus was a promotion.
They had experienced this spiritual power
when Jesus sent them out in poverty (Lk 9):

> "Carry nothing with you
> and do impossible things:
> heal the sick, cast out evil spirits."

And it had worked!
They had actually healed sick people
in the name of Jesus!
They were astounded by this power they had received
that flowed from their very poverty and weakness
enfolded in trust.
They were thrilled at all the miracles Jesus performed;
he even commanded the sea and the winds!
Yes, they admired this powerful Jesus
and were happy to be with him,

to be identified with him and with his power,
to be part of this wonderful, unfolding plan of God.

Jesus chose these twelve men
because he knew (they did not)
that he would not be with them for very long.
He wished to form and transform them,
to prepare them for the role
they would have after he had left.
He was going to empower them
by sending to each one his Spirit
so that they could be good shepherds
for his new flock,
so that they could continue his work
of announcing the good news to the poor
throughout the whole world.
They would be in communion one with another,
parts of the same body,
belonging to the people of God,
centered upon the rock,
Peter,
confirmed by Jesus
to confirm his brothers
and to feed the flock of Jesus.

Jesus formed these men and many other disciples,
not in a formal way
by teaching ideas, skills, or giving them classes in Scripture,
but he formed and transformed them
by living with them,
walking with them,
being a model for them.
He loved them and they loved him
so naturally they learned from him,
to do things as he did them.
He taught them how to live the good news,
how to trust the Father
and to read the signs of God

in all the little events of each day.
He showed them that faith is trust in God,
not ideas about God,
and that this faith and trust grow day by day
through all that is beautiful
as well as through all that is painful,
all that reveals our weakness and poverty.
He showed them that trust is like a dialogue,
a communion
between hearts
that is continually deepening.

Jesus gave them an example of
how to live,
how to love,
how to welcome the poor,
how to become a friend of the powerless,
how to be with women
and with strangers, even with Roman troops,
how to be with sinners, tax collectors,
and victims of prostitution.
They saw how Jesus lived,
simply and poorly,
open to each moment and to each situation,
open to the will of the father,
and how he was moved or motivated
not by a codified, written law,
but by the law of love,
the love of each person in need.

He taught them
as they walked through the fields,
his heart in communion with the heart of God,
hidden in the beauty, harmony, and oneness of nature,
where all things together sing of unity and love.
He had no fixed program of teaching;
he taught them as he looked with love and joy
at the birds of the air, the lilies of the fields,

the sheep and the shepherds,
the grain of wheat,
the sower seeding.
With Jesus, everything they saw and touched and heard
in nature, in the universe, in Scripture,
in the words of the prophets,
all they experienced in and among themselves
and with other people,
became alive and unified.
His teaching was not locked up in ideas and laws,
shut off from the song of birds
or the cry of the poor.
Through his words and presence,
their bodies and their minds,
their hearts,
their faith,
their knowledge of God,
their love of nature and of people,
were unified.
Everything became so clear and easy
as they walked with Jesus.
First of all because he loved them,
he loved each one personally
in a unique way.
Each one felt he was special to Jesus.
He seemed to know each one
with his gifts and his weaknesses.
When they were tired or sick
he was gentle and loving.
At the end of his life, he confessed to them:

> "As the Father loves me
> I love you."

Yes, each one knew that.
They were wrapped in this love,
all that was light and love in them

was called forth
in his loving, truthful presence.

That does not mean that everything was simple
as they lived with Jesus.
There were times
when they did not understand what was going on.
He seemed angry with them
when they tried to stop the children and their mothers
from "pestering" him,
when there were so many other more important people
waiting to speak to him.
He got terribly angry when Peter rebuked him
because he had announced
that he was going to suffer much
and be killed.
The disciples could not understand
the violent reaction of Jesus:
"Get behind me, Satan!" he said to Peter,
to Peter!
the one whom he had just named the rock
upon which the assembly of believers would be built!
And Jesus rebuked them
when they started to argue among themselves
as to who was the most important.

The disciples loved Jesus,
but there were many things
they just could not understand about him:
his body as food?
his blood to drink?
That put everybody off!
Many followers started to leave him
after these seemingly foolish words.
But Jesus seemed so sad, so wounded at their leaving,
as if he had shared with them a deep secret
flowing from his heart
and nobody wanted to listen or to understand.

"Will you also leave me?" Jesus asked his disciples (Jn 6).
One can almost hear the tears in his voice.
The disciples could not understand.

There were many times
when Jesus seemed so sad, so wounded,
with tears in his eyes,
like a a lover, passionately in love,
whose love is rejected by the one he loves.

At other times he became like a child,
with the face and the smile of a little child,
with the poverty, candor, and innocence
of a tiny child
in his eyes and flesh.

Through all he said and did
he seemed to be so free and true
and the disciples loved him for that.
He never sought popularity or votes.
Sometimes his words were harsh,
like when he spoke about
having to hate one's parents
to follow him,
or to take up one's cross,
to love one's enemy,
to leave everything.
They admired him
and were in awe of him.
They loved him,
but they were not sure what he would do next!
He was always doing the unexpected!

Sometimes they were a bit upset with Jesus,
especially when he promised them rest
and then allowed the crowds to overwhelm them (Mk 6).
Could he not see
that they were at the end of their tether?

Among themselves also
it was not always easy.
There were obvious tensions,
particularly around Judas,
who was the most organized of them all
(was that why he was responsible for the finances?)
but certainly not the easiest to live with.
Why couldn't Jesus choose men
who all had the same culture and background?
It would have been so much easier!

But Jesus had called them together
to form community
with him and around him
and with many other disciples, men and women,
a bonding deeper than family ties.
Community where they learned to care for each other,
where each one had his or her place
and gift to exercise,
where they learned also about their brokenness, jealousy,
their desire for power,
and their need for forgiveness and healing,
their need also to forgive;
where they learned continually to be open
to the poor, the lame, the broken, and the blind.
Not a closed community for security,
but a community for healing
and for helping each one to grow in freedom and in love:
a community of mutual support
which announced the good news by its existence
and from which some could go out
to announce the good news of God's love.

Jesus loved these men and women
who had left all to be with him.
Peter wanted to know what recompense they
who had given up everything to follow him
would receive.

> "Truly I say to you,
> Anyone who has left home, brothers, sisters,
> mother, father, children, and fields
> because of me and because of the good news
> will receive even now
> a hundredfold
> in brothers, sisters, mothers, children, and fields,
> with persecutions;
> and in the world to come
> eternal life.
> Many of those who were first
> will be last
> and the last will be first." (Mk 10)

Those who follow Jesus
and give up all for him
will receive all from Jesus.

> "I say these things to you,"
> he said to his followers,
> "so that my joy may be in you
> and that your joy may be total." (Jn 15)

Those Jesus Disturbed

Many people were drawn to Jesus
and found inner healing
and a renewal of hope.
Others were angry with him;
he disturbed them;
he disturbed the rich.
The story of Lazarus and the rich man (Lk 16)
must have disturbed many.
Lazarus was a beggar, his legs covered with sores,
like a leper;
he lay in the street, alone and hungry.
The rich man was giving a lavish party nearby,
ignoring the hungry look in the eyes of Lazarus.

Lazarus died and entered into the land of peace,
inside Abraham;
when the rich man died
he entered the place of torment.
What clearer message could there be?

Jesus cried out:

> "Woe unto you the rich,
> you are filled now,
> you laugh and have fun;
> you are honored and admired!" (Lk 6)

Some were obviously angry with him
because they thought he was making them feel guilty.
It was not that Jesus did not love them or care for them,
far from that.
All he wanted was to open their hearts and minds,
to free them from their addiction to possessions
and their need for wealth,
and to show them the way to inner freedom,
the path to sharing and compassion.
To close oneself behind the barriers of wealth and class,
to hide among the so-called elite,
is a form of death;
to refuse our common humanity and solidarity
with those who cry out their needs and pain,
to refuse to share our lives and wealth
with those who have less
is a form of death.

Jesus did not tell rich people like
Zacchaeus of Jericho (Lk 19)
to sell everything they had.
All he asked was that they open their houses and families
to hospitality and to compassion,
and not be afraid.
He called them to open their hearts,
and not to hide from the weak, the powerless, the needy,

but to share with them,
to share their lives, their food, their wealth.
It is then that they shall find new life,
they will find God,
they will find happiness,
they will be blest.

That is why he told a Pharisee,

> "When you give a lunch or a supper,
> do not invite your family, your rich neighbors,
> nor your rich friends;
> but when you give a banquet
> invite the poor, the lame, the blind, and the crippled
> and you shall be blest.
> God will be with you." (Lk 14)

But so many of the rich and powerful
were unable to change;
they did not want to change;
they did not want to invite
the poor, the crippled, and the lame to their table;
they were frightened of losing control.
Closed in on themselves
and on their religious prejudices,
they could not stand the smell of the rabble,
the stench of the lepers and the sick,
the cry of the beggars.
They refused to listen to the wisdom of the women
and of the weak.
They were at ease with the established order,
with the high priest and the religious leaders
who did not disturb them
but flattered them instead.
And they flattered each other:
the club of the powerful and the elite.
They criticized the dirty, motley, uncouth crowd,
and the radical so-called prophet,
who befriended the powerless, the forsaken, and the dirty,

who touched the lepers,
spoke gently to Samaritans,
listened to women,
and even let his feet be washed by the tears
of a woman of ill repute.

So too Jesus disturbed
the angry, jealous poor and powerless,
locked in their despair
and feelings of revolt,
angry with God and with religion,
angry with their lot,
angry with the prophets.
Yes, they were angry with Jesus
who spoke of trust
instead of revolt.
They avoided Jesus
or were furious with him
if he did not give them alms
or heal them on their own terms.
So too Jesus disturbed those men and women
locked in their ways
of drink and debauchery
who had cut themselves off from the laws of God
and did not want to hear anything about love
and forgiveness.

He disturbed some whom he looked at
with love (Mk 10)
and called them,
invited them,
to follow him
in trust,
to sell all they had,
to let go,
and to walk humbly with him
as a friend.
They felt unable to choose,

unable to accept the loss
of wealth, family, position, self-image,
which gave a certain meaning and security to their lives.
They did not dare take the step into the insecurity
of a new love and a deeper trust.
He disturbed,
worried,
and saddened them.

Jesus disturbed those who found him
too radical,
utopian,
unrealistic.
How can one give up wealth and share with the poor?
How can one renounce violence?
How can one love one's enemy?
How can one forgive and forgive?
How can one live without security and money?
How can one become like a little child?
How can one eat his flesh and drink his blood?
Those who questioned and questioned
and wanted to understand,
refusing to wait,
those who could not fit his ways and teachings
into their own ideas,
refused to trust him,
and turned away.
They found it impossible, unreasonable, dangerous
to accept the newness of his message.
They needed to conform to the system
and to the established traditions,
to obey religious authority without questioning it.

Jesus disturbed all those who refused to admit
their poverty, brokenness, and sinfulness,
their need for help,
those who closed themselves up
in their knowledge, wealth,

and spiritual power,
who justified themselves,
judging and accusing others.

Perhaps Jesus disturbed everybody!
He shattered expectations
and aroused anger.
It is normal that a prophet disturb.

Some who were disturbed waited;
they lived inner hurts,
feelings of anguish and guilt,
but they did not close the door
or turn away.
Others closed themselves up
in their own pain
and pride;
they refused to listen
and turned away angry with Jesus
and with themselves.
Still others went even further
and tried to destroy Jesus,
to hurt him
and those who followed him.

And above all, Jesus disturbed the established order:
the Sadducees, the Pharisees, the scribes,
the high priest, and the religious leaders.
Not all of them.
Some were touched by his message and ways
and by the signs of God so clearly manifested.
They came to see him by night,
like Nicodemus,
or they invited him to their homes.
Nicodemus even defended him publicly
but was quickly attacked for that (Jn 7).
They were open to him and to his message,
but were frightened of being publicly identified with him.

They could not commit the institution
of which they were part
and which had its own ways
of judging and of making decisions.
Like so many in religious groups over the centuries,
they were frightened of appearing different,
of not conforming to the established group
that had power;
frightened of criticism and of dishonor,
frightened of trusting
and following their own conscience,
they had lost their inner freedom.

The majority of them were clearly angry with Jesus
and refused to listen to him.
They were closed up
in their own ways, doctrines, and ideology.
Jesus could *not* be the Messiah!
He could *not* be from God!
He could not work signs;
if he did, they were surely signs made by Satan,
to fool the crowds
and lead the gullible rabble astray.

They were even unable to listen to Jesus,
or to recognize that a tree
is to be judged by its fruits.
They condemned Jesus
even before *looking* at the fruits
of his life, his work,
and his message.
They were fixed in their prejudices and pride,
or unconsciously frightened
of their own anguish and guilt
hidden under the cloak of spiritual power
and exterior values,
protected by the establishment.

And why this prejudice?

One has to admit that no group
likes to have a prophet rise up
in its midst,
even religious groups.
A prophet reveals something new,
a new road
not seen by the group;
the prophet implicitly reveals
the poverty, the incapacity, and the darkness of the group.
Sometimes prophets even announce clearly
that the group has deviated
from its initial aim and vision;
that it has closed itself off
in comfort, self-satisfaction, and human security;
that it has lost the love and enthusiasm
of its younger days;
that it has lost trust in God
and is fearful of poverty and insecurity,
which are like a sacrament
calling anew for the presence and help of God.

A group is quickly suspicious and frightened
of the new,
frightened of a prophet,
who has the power to undermine its own authority.
A group resists change;
leaders are fearful of losing control.

Some of the religious leaders in Israel
during the time of Jesus
felt this fear.
Perhaps unconsciously they were fearful of being revealed
in all their hypocrisy and inner emptiness.
They had all the external trappings of religiosity
and of the knowledge of God,
but inside they were empty;

in the harsh, clear words of Jesus
they were filled with "rapacity and dead bones,"
like whitened sepulchres.

In a very public, open way,
Jesus revealed the evil in them.
He said openly what many people knew and thought
but dared to say only in whispers.
He called them snakes, brood of vipers,
hypocrites, blind guides (Mt 23),
who closed the doors of the Kingdom to people,
who paid small taxes and performed little rituals
but forgot about the essential,
which is justice and mercy and faith.
He harangued them, shouted at them,
making comparisons in his parables
that embarrassed and enraged them (Lk 10).
He spoke of the priest and the Levite
who did not stop on the road to Jericho
to help the man lying in pain;
they were frightened of becoming impure
by touching his wounds;
the Samaritan, the stranger, the heretic,
the so-called cursed one,
did stop.
The lesson was clear.
It is not because a man is a priest,
fulfilling the rituals of the Law,
that he is closer to God:
closeness to God comes from love and openness
and caring for one's neighbor.
The first commandment is to love the Lord
with all one's heart, spirit, mind, and strength,
and to love one's neighbor as oneself.
That is the heart of the Torah.

So too in the parable
of the Pharisee and the publican (Lk 18).

The Pharisee stands up front in the Temple
proclaiming all the good things he has done,
how he had fulfilled the Law,
and even more;
he gives thanks that he is not like other men,
particularly the publican.
The publican stands far away at the back,
not daring to lift up his eyes to heaven,
striking his breast and saying:
"O God, have mercy on me, a sinner."
And Jesus says that it is this publican
who goes away justified, held in the love of God,
and not the Pharisee.
No wonder they wanted to get rid of Jesus!
He was a threat to them
and to their influence and power.
He revealed their inner poverty and brokenness.

In another instance,
the Pharisees and scribes said they could not believe
Jesus was the Messiah
because he came from Galilee (Jn 7);
people from Judea and Jerusalem despised the Galileans
who observed the Law with less rigor.
Jesus had not grown up in the system;
he was an outsider, unlearned according to their norms.
Besides he could *not* be the Messiah
because he broke the laws of the Sabbath
(those laws that did not come from God).
He could not be the Messiah because,
because...
because...
They tried to trap him on every possible occasion
to prove to themselves — and to the people —
that he was not a faithful disciple of Moses,
thus he could not be the Messiah.
They *did not want* him to be the Messiah;

he was too threatening,
threatening to their power
and to the system.
And clearly he claimed equality to God;
he claimed to *be* God.
This, they cried out, was the ultimate blasphemy,
punishable by death.

We human beings have an amazing capacity
to deny reality,
to refuse reality,
and to close ourselves up
in our own ideas, theories, and prejudices,
in what *we* want reality to be.
We human beings have difficulty
in being really open to reality,
seeking knowledge that springs from it;
we want reality to conform to our own ideas;
we want to fabricate reality
rather than to submit.
So it was with many of the Pharisees and the scribes.

Those in the system,
protected by the system,
privileged by and in the system,
bonded together in loyalty to the establishment,
with its laws and order,
can quickly deny reality
and refuse to judge a tree by its fruits.
They see Jesus as a threat.
The establishment had a clear power structure:
at the top, the Sanhedrin, the high priest,
the scribes and the elders
who were in control;
at the bottom, the unlearned of the Law, the uncouth,
the so-called gullible, the naive, the women,
the lowly, the lepers, the sick, the mad,
those with handicaps;

at the top, the wealthy and the powerful;
at the bottom, the poor and the powerless.

Jesus was attracting all kinds of people:
especially the lowly, the lawless, the uncouth;
"even prostitutes and sinners"
were flocking to him,
recognizing in him a prophet.
How could he be the Messiah?

Jesus was beginning to rock the boat
and to threaten the system and its values.
If people who were voiceless and powerless
started to feel they had religious rights
and should have a say in things,
then a whole transformation would start to take place.
The poor, the rabble, should be kept in their place;
women should be kept silent.
If not, there would be trouble.
The leaders would no longer be in control,
at least not in the same way.
And, of course, they thought the Romans
would react to this
(and maybe they were right!).
Pontius Pilate and his troops
might then destroy the nation,
take away from the leaders those rights and privileges
that they had been allowed to keep.
These leaders had a lot to lose;
they were not able to accept the threat of loss.
Jesus was becoming dangerous;
he should be eliminated, killed.

> "Do you not understand,"
> said the chief priest,
> "that one man must die
> to save the whole nation?" (Jn 11)

He did not realize how right he was.

But how to get rid of Jesus?
How to kill him?
Only the representatives of the emperor
had the power to condemn to death.
How to catch hold of Jesus
and to arrest him?
If the priests sent the soldiers of the Temple
to take hold of Jesus
in broad daylight,
the people might revolt;
they loved Jesus and saw in him
a prophet sent by God.
The priests needed a traitor
who would show them where Jesus spent the night.
Then they could send soldiers
to arrest him
in secret.

Judas Iscariot,
one of the twelve men
chosen by Jesus,
was this traitor.
Judas had walked with Jesus,
had listened to him,
had witnessed his goodness and power.
Judas was loved by Jesus.
However, he had hidden from the others
his unease and ambivalent feelings
about Jesus.
They never suspected
that he could betray Jesus.

Judas went to the priests of the Temple
and offered to show them
where Jesus would be at night.
The priests were delighted

and gave him thirty pieces of silver (Mk 26, Lk 22)
for this dirty work.

During the last supper
Judas left after Jesus had washed his feet
with love and humility;
Satan had entered into his heart (Jn 13).
The group of soldiers was waiting.
Judas led them quietly through the night (Lk 22)
to where Jesus was praying
in agony
in the Garden of Gethsemane.
He went up to Jesus and kissed him.
He had told the soldiers that the one he would kiss
was Jesus of Nazareth,
the one to be taken away.

Thus with a kiss
Judas betrayed Jesus
and gave him up to be killed.
He gave Jesus up to be killed.

Why this violent act,
this horrible, despicable gesture?
Only jealousy can lead someone to such a thing.
Judas is consumed with jealousy!

He must have both loved and hated Jesus.
He must have wanted Jesus
all for himself.
He wanted to be the only one for Jesus,
a broken child screaming out for a father
but ambivalent about the father.

Judas was certainly jealous of Mary, the sister of Martha;
his attitude in Bethany reveals this (Jn 11).
He was also jealous of John "the beloved one"
reclining on the breast of Jesus
at the last meal (Jn 13).

Judas needed to prove that he was someone;
he wanted power;
he wanted to be that indispensable
supporter of Jesus,
helping him to succeed
politically and religiously.
Judas certainly did not want a weak Jesus,
the Jesus of compassion
and communion.
Judas was a terribly broken man,
filled with anguish,
unable to let go and to put his trust in Jesus.
Anguish is the soil
in which Satan delights.
From anguish can arise horrible jealousy,
hatred,
terrible acts inspired by the Evil One.

Once this vile act of betrayal is accomplished,
Judas finds himself alone,
despised by everyone,
despised by his own self,
sick with anguish and guilt.
He commits suicide,
hanging himself from a tree (Mk 27).
But as the rope tightened around his neck,
his legs dangling in the air,
perhaps he remembered
the compassionate, forgiving face of Jesus,
tears in his eyes.

IV

THE DESCENT OF JESUS INTO PAIN AND LITTLENESS _____

When his hour had come
Jesus was clothed in still greater weakness;
he descended into the pit of pain and littleness.

In his letter to the disciples in Philippi,
Paul quotes what seems to have been
one of the earliest hymns sung by Christians.

> He who was in the form of God
> (the eternal Word)
> did not count equality to God
> a thing to be clutched to
> but *he emptied himself*
> taking on the form of a slave,
> being born in the likeness of human beings.
> And being found in human form
> he humbled himself still more
> and became obedient unto death,
> even death on a cross. (Phil 2)

In the face of the danger in Jerusalem
Jesus does not hide away
nor flee to Galilee.

Jesus, the gentle, innocent one
allows himself to be encircled by the forces of evil
and to be captured,
bound up with ropes
and led away,
firmly held between brutal soldiers
with their violent ways.

He came unto his own
but his own received him not;
they did not want him as he was.
His gentle, forgiving love,
his quiet call to become like little children,
his meekness and non-violence,
his appeal to take the last place
are shoved violently aside by the powerful system,
impenetrable to tenderness
like heavy concrete bunkers.
Here is the ultimate opposition:
a little child,
innocent,
crying out for love and tenderness and truth,
revealing to these men, prisoners of the system,
blocked by anguish, fear, lies, and pride,
by their own prejudices, hate, darkness, fear,
and certainty of righteousness,
their frightened, sinful hearts, transformed into stone.

The light in Jesus,
the truth he speaks,
seem to awaken the darkness,
the world of lies,
in each one.
His gentle love reveals
their violence;
his purity,
their dirt;
his humble way

produces a powerful reaction of pride.
Since he does not correspond to the idea many have
of the powerful Messiah
who would liberate and bring an earthly paradise,
he was a disappointment:
"He has deceived us."
The inner violence of many people in the crowd
surges up
as they spit their wrath,
they who a few days before cried out
as Jesus entered Jerusalem:

> "Hosanna, hosanna, Son of David,
> King of Israel!"

now cry out:

> "Crucify him! Crucify him!"

Jesus reveals the sinfulness,
the evil,
and the darkness
within the hearts of human beings.
This is unbearable for them.
They accuse him,
scream at him,
deny and hide their own evil,
which they project upon him.
He becomes the scapegoat
and the victim
of their evil.

Jesus is pushed into the pit
of weakness and humiliation,
failure and abandonment,
encircled by darkness.

His friends, his chosen ones,
those he had sought to form and transform
as they walked the paths of Galilee together
and sailed on the lake,

are confused,
terrified;
they break down,
run away,
abandon Jesus to his fate.
Peter, the "rock," collapses,
swearing, shouting, cursing, crying out:
"I do not know this man!" (Mt 26).

He had known and followed the powerful Jesus,
the Jesus of miracles,
the Jesus who fed the five thousand,
who raised Lazarus from the dead,
who was transfigured on the mountain.
His hope was in the powerful Messiah
sent by God
to win the struggle between good and evil
(and clearly evil was in the Romans),
to rid the land of pagan domination,
refind dignity, fervor, and hope
in the chosen people
and restore the Kingdom of Israel.

But now all is over.
Jesus is overpowered;
he has lost the struggle;
he will be eliminated
like others before him.
Peter's inner world breaks down;
his own anguish and violence rise up.
He falls into confusion and inner chaos.
That is why he curses and says:
"I do not know this man!"
This is not the man he has followed,
in whom he has put all his trust,
the Messiah of power,
the servant of the *Almighty*,
the one who had to win.

Peter cannot understand;
it is as if Jesus has cheated him.
For him weakness is akin to cowardice;
it has no meaning.
Men are called to fight and to struggle,
to compete and to win.
And the best will always win,
blessed by God
and with God's power.

Peter cannot understand
the hidden, humble message of the prophet,
the suffering servant announced by Isaiah (53):

> "Like a lamb brought to the slaughter
> he opened not his mouth...
> Yet by his wounds we are healed."

Peter could not bear failure and dishonor.
He ran away,
a broken man.
How can failure prepare for success?
Death bring life?

Yet in nature
fallen, dying leaves,
human and animal excrement,
all that is rejected and decaying,
enrich the soil
and give life.
What is most rejected
becomes most precious,
just as the dirtiest
becomes the cleanest:
putrid apples and grapes
transformed into alcohol.
Jesus had said:

> "Unless a grain of wheat
> which falls into the earth

>dies, it remains alone;
>if it dies,
>it bears much fruit." (Jn 12)

Jesus descends into the dark earth
of weakness, humiliation, and abandonment.
There he will bear much fruit.

This weakness of Jesus is not just physical;
he is shattered in the depths of his being.
Before his arrest
in the garden of olives (Mk 14, Lk 22)
near the walls of Jerusalem,
he took three of his most loved companions
and asked them to watch and pray with him.
Overwhelmed with inner pain,
crushed with sadness,
inwardly shattered,
prostrate in agony,
sweat flowing from all the pores of his skin,
like blood,
he wept,
deeply troubled,
praying:

>"Abba, Daddy, little Father
>may this chalice,
>this excruciating inner pain,
>pass from me,
>but not my will,
>yours be done."

He could not stand the pain of abandonment,
rejection, and utter failure;
he cried out for strength.
The desolation and littleness of Jesus
crying out for love
yet surrendered to love.

> The soldiers took him inside
> the governor's residence, the Praetorium,
> and called the whole cohort together.
> They dressed him up in purple,
> twisted some thorns into a crown
> and put it on him.
> And they began saluting him,
> "Hail king of the Jews!"
> They struck his head with a reed
> and spat on him, and they went down
> on their knees to do him homage. (Mk 15)

The soldiers laughed sadistically
at his weakness
and beat him up,
enjoying his pain.

Then he lay dishonored,
totally naked on the cross,
his beautiful, delicate body
wounded, gashed, bloody,
crucified,
exposed to all the curious.
The Pharisees and the scribes revelled
in his nakedness and weakness,
his groaning and his pain.
They had won.
They were the strong ones.
He had lost.
They laughed, jeered, and mocked him.

> The chief priests with the scribes and elders
> mocked him with the words
> "He saved others; he cannot save himself.
> He is the king of Israel; let him come down
> from the cross now, and we will believe him."
>
> (Mt 27)

But he opened not his mouth to them,
just tears,
quiet tears:

> "Forgive them, Father,
> for they know not what they are doing." (Lk 23)

The pain,
the excruciating pain,
the weight of his body
hanging by its arms
nailed to the wood,
unable to breathe with ease.
To take in a little air
he had to push up with his legs
and his nailed feet,
otherwise it was the agony of asphyxiation,
his voice barely a whisper.

Nailed to the cross,
naked, stripped of everything,
abandoned by his friends
who had lost trust in him,
dishonored in his mission
and in his manhood,
Jesus nevertheless remains in communion
with Mary, his mother.
She was the one who had lived with him,
his primary and fundamental relationship;
she was the first to welcome him
in his littleness
the day of his conception.
She is standing there at the foot of the cross
next to his broken, naked, wounded body,
holding his weakness
in trust, in compassion, and in love,
in total gift of herself,
one with him,
offered with him

in sacrifice to the Father,
her broken heart
dissolved in his broken heart.

And in an ultimate act of love,
Jesus gives away this visible communion with her,
the woman.
He tells her not to look at him
but at John.

"Woman, behold your son."

And to John:

"Here is your mother." (Jn 19)

As she turns to look at the beloved disciple
Jesus now alone,
totally alone,
in anguish cries:

"I thirst" (Jn 19)

"Eli, Eli, lema sabachthani?"
"My God, my God, why have you abandoned me?"
(Mt 27)

Then he gives up his spirit.
The final cry of pain and anguish.
All is over.

"All is consummated." (Jn 19)

His breathing stopped.
His body became limp and still.
Jesus is dead.

⌘

Crucified outside the walls of Jerusalem,
the city of God,
excommunicated
by the legal representatives of God,
damned as a blasphemer
(a clear sign that he was not of God):

no comeliness nor beauty in him (see Is 53),
a man of sorrow,
familiar with suffering,
crushed for our sins,
the sacrificed lamb of God.
He gave his life;
he gave us life,
opening up the floodgates of living waters
waiting to be spread over the earth.
From his heart pierced by the soldier's spear
flowed blood and water (Jn 19).
A gentle Savior.
A little Lamb.
Through his death he gave life
to the world,
and conquered evil, the power of Satan,
transforming the violence of the world
into tenderness and forgiveness.

Yes, he loved
to the fulfillment of love,
to the very end of love,
to the total gift of himself,
showing us how God loves.

The man of compassion,
with spiritual power,
had become the powerless man
in need of compassion.
The man who had announced good news to the poor,
liberty and freedom to the oppressed,
had become the impoverished man
chained in sadness.
The man who had cried out in the Temple:
"Let anyone who thirsts come to me and drink"
now cried out in pain: "I thirst!"
The man who came to heal
was in need of healing.

The man who came to give love
had become desperately in need of love:
the teacher, the model of compassion,
cried out for compassion.
The man who came to give life
and life in abundance
died in cruel emptiness and pain.

They took his dead body down from the cross,
removed the nails,
and laid it on the lap of his mother,
Mary.
Mary, the compassionate one,
was with him in the ecstasy of conception,
enveloping the Word made flesh in her.
She was with him
at birth
as he left her body
to be enfolded in her arms,
to rest on her breasts.
She is with him now in death,
enfolding his limp body,
the Woman enfolding Man
in tenderness.
She holds and touches his sacred body,
sacrament of God:
her gift to God,
God's gift to her.

There she waits:
her beloved son,
her only son,
the beloved son,
only son
of the Father,
resting, dead,
upon her own sacrificed heart.

All is over.
Nothing,
nothing is left;
the crowds disperse;
his friends are afraid,
only humiliation, distress, agony, mockery,
and her love and trust remain.

She waits,
believing,
trusting:
three times he had said to his followers
that he would suffer much,
be killed,
and on the third day rise up.

What could this mean
at this moment of total, utter failure,
when the forces of jealousy and evil,
in the name of religion,
in the name of God,
have silenced the living Word of God?
Yet Mary waits.

She teaches us to wait.
We poor humans are caught in prisons of our making,
in impossible situations,
conflicting desires
that paralyze us,
and cause us to wait in depression and closed silence,
in agitation and in revolt,
as we seek to forget.

As the body of Jesus is taken from her
he descends,
always descending
into the silent night
of the tomb.
The stone is put over its mouth.

All is silent.
All is over.

Mary,
the martyred woman,
her heart too pierced by the sword (Lk 2),
as announced by Simeon,
is gently held and accompanied
by John,
the beloved disciple of Jesus,
who has taken her as his own mother.

She waits.

While the group of disciples argue,
broken, confused, despairing,
Judas has hung himself.
Peter is ashamed and angry with everyone,
and above all with himself;
he is no longer the rock.
Two of them cut themselves off
from the squabbling group
and head for Emmaus (Lk 24).

V

JESUS LIVES _____

At the first inklings of light
on the Sunday morning,
Mary of the Roman camp of Magdala (Jn 20)
prepares to run to the tomb
where they have laid the limp, silent body
of her beloved.
She is angry with Peter
and with all those frightened men,
incompetent cowards,
more concerned with themselves
and the failure of their mission
to restore the Kingdom
than with Jesus
and his pain.
Mary is alone in her pain;
she could seek solace
only in the one she loved.
Courageous and beautiful Mary,
energized by love
and the desire to see and touch
the body of her beloved.

But the tomb is empty!

> "Where is my Lord?"
> "Who has taken his body?"
> "Where is he?"

She weeps and screams her pain.

Running wildly,
fragmented, dispersed,
anguished,

> "Where is he?
> Where is his body?"

Suddenly, near the empty tomb
she sees a man whom she mistakes for the gardener.
Maybe it is he who has taken away the body
of her Lord.
"Mary," he says with love
and looks at her
as he had always looked at her:
It is Jesus
alive!

> "Rabboni!
> O Beloved!
> It is you!"

Her heart pounding,
she rushes to clasp him
and touch his feet,
those feet she had anointed with love
in Bethany.
But he says:

> "Do not touch me
> for I have not yet gone to the Father.
> But go and find my brothers
> and tell them
> I go to my Father and your Father,
> to my God and your God."

No, she must not touch him
or hold on to him.
Yes, it is Jesus,
but he is different,
not raised like her brother, Lazarus;

his body is the same
yet not the same.
The risen Jesus will no longer meet her in the same way
physically,
externally.
He will meet her within.
She must discover this new form of presence
hidden in her own heart of flesh.

Jesus descended into the pangs of death,
the night of the tomb,
to rise up,
living
in a totally new way,
his risen, glorious body
not limited by space or time.

The early Christians' hymn,
the *kenosis*, the emptying,
becomes a song of humble triumph.

> And for this God raised him high,
> and gave him the name
> which is above all names;
> so that all beings
> in the heavens, on earth, and in the underworld
> should bend the knee at the name of Jesus
> and that every tongue should acknowledge
> Jesus Christ as Lord
> to the glory of the Father. (Phil 2)

The resurrection of Jesus
is the most stupendous cosmic reality
in the history of our universe
but yet so humble.
Jesus does not appear in triumph
over the Temple of Jerusalem,
humiliating those who had humiliated him.
He appears to his friends,

those whom he has chosen,
in quiet humility.
They are terrified,
taking him for a ghost!

> "No, it is me,
> it is really me!
> Touch me,
> look at me,
> give me something to eat." (Lk 24)

They cannot understand.
It is difficult for them to believe.
They are like us,
so slow of heart,
so slow to believe.

The gentle, risen Jesus
does not reproach them for their cowardice;
he does not admonish them for having abandoned him.
He does, however, reproach them
for not believing the woman,
Mary of the Roman camp,
when she announced to them
that she had seen him alive (Mk 16).

But it *is* true.
It *is* Jesus
alive,
the same body,
yet different!
"My Lord and my God!"
cries Thomas
transformed in hope and in joy
as he puts his fingers
into the wounds in Jesus' hands and feet
and his hand into Jesus' side,
which had been cut open by the lance (Jn 20).

From total, utter collapse and failure
something totally and utterly new has arisen,
the unexpected,
the humble risen Christ
alive,
giving courage to the broken,
renewing hope,
giving life,
empowering them.

Yes, Jesus is gentle;
there is no harshness in him.
He walked on the road to Emmaus (Lk 24)
with those two men
who were fleeing in despair and anger
from the broken community of the disciples.
Hiding his wounds he asks them
what they are talking about.

> "Are you the only person in Jerusalem
> not to have heard the news
> of what has happened?"
> "What news?" he asks.

They tell him about Jesus and his death.
And Jesus reveals to them the secret of the Scriptures.
Their hearts begin to burn in ecstasy.
But they recognize him
only when he blesses and breaks the bread
during the evening meal.
Then Jesus disappears.

Later, in Galilee (Jn 21),
from the shore of the lake,
Jesus calls out to the disciples
who are fishing:

> "Hey, children, have you caught anything?"
> "No," they answer.
> "Throw out your nets on the right side."

When they do that,
their nets are filled with fish.
They rush ashore, recognizing Jesus.
He invites them to breakfast.
Such a gentle, risen Jesus
concerned with the welfare
of his hungry disciples! (Jn 21)

After breakfast Jesus asks Peter three times
"Do you love me?"
Peter is embarrassed
for he remembers how he denied Jesus three times.
Peter is more humble now:
"You know I love you," he tells Jesus.
Then Jesus confirms him as the rock:

> "Feed my lambs,
> tend my sheep."

Yes, Peter, in all his weakness,
remains the shepherd
called to confirm others.

Over forty days Jesus appeared at different times
to his disciples,
who, through this experience of brokenness,
had become poorer
and more humble,
more anchored in reality.
He spoke to them about the Kingdom of God,
preparing thus the birth of the Church,
his body,
preparing them to continue the work he had begun:
to go down the ladder of human promotion
to announce all over the world
the message of forgiveness and universal love,
good news for the poor,
and to baptize
in the name of the Father, the Son, and the Holy Spirit,

bringing new life,
a rebirth,
for those who trust and want renewal
in truth.

He promised them they would receive
a new force (Lk 24; Jn 14, 16),
the Holy Spirit,
the Spirit of Jesus,
the Paraclete,
sent by his Father.
She would transform them,
nourish them,
and teach them all things,
to become like Jesus,
true shepherds of the flock.

> Then during a meal that he shared with them
> he told them not to leave Jerusalem,
> but to wait there
> for what the Father had promised.
> "It is," he said,
> "what you have heard me speak about:
> John baptized with water,
> but not many days from now
> you are going to be baptized
> with the Holy Spirit. . . .
> You will receive the power of the Holy Spirit
> which will come on you,
> and then you will be my witnesses,
> not only in Jerusalem
> but throughout Judea and Samaria
> and indeed to earth's remotest end."
> And as he said this, he was lifted up
> while they looked on,
> and a cloud took him from their sight.
> They were staring into the sky as he went,
> when suddenly two men in white

were standing beside them and they said,
"Why are you Galileans standing here
looking into the sky?
This Jesus
who has been taken from you into heaven
will come back in the same way
as you have seen him
go to heaven." (Acts 1)

So it was that ten days later,
on the feast of Pentecost,
the Holy Spirit descended upon them
as they were praying together with one heart,
with Mary, the mother of Jesus,
and a few other women.
Like tongues of fire,
the Spirit appeared over each one.
Each was then reborn
into a new force,
their hearts burning with the force of love.
This fire filled some with a yearning
for deeper silence and prayer
and others a yearning to announce Jesus and his vision
with renewed courage
and in many languages.
All who witnessed this event and heard them speak
were amazed (Acts 2).

Peter, filled with the Holy Spirit,
stood up and announced with force
a new era of love
as he cited the words of the prophet Joel.

"In the last days, the Lord declares,
I shall pour out my Spirit on all humanity.
Your sons and daughters shall prophesy,
your young people shall see visions,
your old people dream dreams.
Even on the slaves, men and women,

shall I pour out my Spirit.
I will show portents in the sky above
and signs on the earth below.
The sun will be turned into darkness
and the moon into blood
before the day of the Lord comes,
that great and terrible Day.
And all who call on the name of the Lord
shall be saved." (Acts 2)

The death and resurrection of Jesus
have shattered the barriers
that prevented the Spirit of God from flowing.
The floodgates are now open.
The Spirit of God,
the Spirit of Jesus,
is given directly to human hearts,
which now become the abode of God.
With the grace of the Holy Spirit,
freed from fear and sin,
hands can now be held across frontiers and cultures;
communion with the risen Jesus
becomes the strength and binding force
of all people, from all nations and all races.

The risen Jesus who ascended into heaven,
to the Father,
one with the Father,
sends to all people
the gift of his Holy Spirit,
a gift that is offered, not imposed,
a gift given to those who search humbly
and cry out their trust.
Transformed by this gift of the Spirit
all can now enter into communion
with Jesus and with the Father
and truly become children of God,
a love flowing from the Trinity,

bringing people into the life of the Trinity.
So we become like Jesus,
are transformed into him.
We receive his Spirit,
his heart in our heart,
loving each person as Jesus loves,
just as they are,
whether they be weak or strong,
the same or different.
We discover the presence of Jesus
hidden within them,
healing us.
We discover suffering
as a sacrament,
the place where Jesus resides.

Jesus had clearly shown
how he would live in his disciples
who together become the Church,
his body, his Temple;
until the end of the world
he would be with those who trust in him
and believe in him:

> "I am the Vine,
> my Father the Vine-dresser...
> and you are the branches.
> The person who abides in me
> and I in that person
> bears much fruit.
> Apart from me, you can do nothing.
> By this my Father is glorified
> that you bear much fruit
> and so prove to be my disciples." (Jn 15)

But this transformation is never instantaneous.
The branches of the vine must be cut and pruned
in order to bear more fruit.
It is a process of growth,

a purifying and liberating process.
We grow in the Spirit,
in wisdom and in freedom and in love,
through crises, pain, and struggle,
fidelity and joy,
through time.
And thus the assembly of those who are called to believe,
the people of God,
born and united in the Spirit,
the Church of Jesus, his body, his people
is born.

The role of the twelve men chosen by Jesus
will be different
from the role of priests according to Jewish law.
They will be called to bring
the words and life of Jesus,
the body of Jesus,
to the poor, the lowly, the oppressed,
the crippled, and the blind,
to all those who cry out their trust.
Jesus had told them
to do in memory of him (Mt 26; Mk 14; Lk 22)
what he had done the night before he died
when he took bread
and blessed it
and broke it
and gave it to each one:

>"Take and eat all of you
>for this is my body."

And when he took the chalice of wine
blessed it and said,

>"Take and drink
>for this is the chalice of my blood,
>the blood of the new and everlasting covenant

which shall be shed for you and for many
for the forgiveness of sins."
Those words that had turned away so many
that day in Galilee
now become presence and mystery,
silence and communion,
as these men announce them
over bread and wine,
revealing sacred mysteries
enfolded in contemplation.

These words take on new meaning:
Jesus remains present among his believers,
present in his body and his blood,
the place of thanksgiving,
the Eucharist,
where again all is offered
and sacrifice becomes a place of communion and gift,
total exchange between the human and the divine
where our flesh
is embraced by the Word made flesh.

VI

CONCLUSION _____

With the Word becoming flesh,
with God taking on a human form,
able to be touched, held, and listened to,
all things are changed;
something totally new is given to our world.

Before the Word became flesh
there was always tension
between flesh and spirit,
body and soul.
To approach God, Infinite Spirit,
Eternal Being,
separated from all matter,
one had to seek a certain separation from one's own body,
which was often seen as the "prison of the soul"
and the place of dangerous instincts and passions.
To approach God, Source of all being,
Supreme Wisdom and Intelligence,
one had to become intelligent and powerful.
Those who were powerless and foolish
were distanced from God.

Other peoples, inspired by God,
saw and touched God
in the beauty, power, and life of the universe;
they saw the face of God
living, moving, singing

in the body of the universe,
but this was hardly a personal God.

With the Word becoming flesh
all things are changed.
Jesus makes all things new.
The Word became flesh
precisely to be close to the foolish and the powerless,
to the weak,
to all those who do not have the inner energy or power
to walk up the mountain of holiness.
He comes to touch hearts,
to call people to trust,
and to be in communion with him.
He calls every person into a new order,
a body of love
where the weak are at the center,
and no longer in a hierarchy of power
where the weak are at the bottom,
held down and crushed.

As the Word becomes flesh
a new unity is created
between flesh and spirit,
body and soul,
through and in and with the power of the Holy Spirit,
who unites all things
and brings all things into oneness
and wholeness.

The Word Who Became Flesh Leads Us on the Downward Path of Humility

The Word became flesh and weakness
so that human beings would not be afraid of God.
"Be not afraid"
is repeated by the prophets and by Jesus.
The Word became a little, powerless child,

a crucified, powerless man
in the arms of Mary,
in order to enter into communion with us,
the to-and-fro of love,
"Emmanuel," "God-with-us."
The strong and the rich do not need others;
they are sufficient unto themselves.
The weak are always in need of others,
calling others forth to communion and community.
The Word became flesh and weakness
to empower us with love,
to melt our hardness,
to break down our inner barriers and systems of defense,
which protect our vulnerability
and behind which we hide our loneliness and fears.
He came to touch us in the core of our being,
to awaken and cleanse the deepest energies
hidden within us,
energies made for love and compassion,
to give life.
The early Christians sang about the descent of the Word
into poverty and littleness.
Paul asks his disciples to have the same desire:
to follow Jesus on the path of humility (Phil 2).

We have already spoken of how Jesus
became the little one,
entering into the pit of pain.
During the paschal meal,
the night before he died,
he got up from the table,
took off his clothes,
and, dressed only in the underwear of a slave,
began to wash his disciples' feet,
taking the role of the servant, the slave (Jn 13).

His disciples, surprised and shocked
as Jesus took off his clothes,

were even more shocked by this gesture.
Peter refused.

> "You shall not wash my feet, never."
> "If I cannot wash your feet,
> our friendship is broken,
> there will no more sharing between us,"
> answered Jesus.

Peter let Jesus wash his feet.
But somehow he could not bear
to have his feet washed by the Lord and Master.
He would gladly wash the feet of Jesus
but not the other way round.
Jesus was creating a new order,
destroying the recognized hierarchy
of authority and power.
If Peter let Jesus wash his feet
then he in turn would have to wash the feet
of those under him
and not expect them to wash his feet!
He too would have to take on the role
of the servant or slave.
The world had suddenly been turned upside down.

Having washed their feet,
Jesus explained the gesture to them:

> "If I have washed your feet
> you must wash one another's feet.
> I have done this as an example for you.
> If you do this
> you will be blessed.
> God will be with you."

Through this gesture of love, communion,
service, and forgiveness,
touching their bodies with love,
Jesus reveals a new vision of authority.
If he, the Lord and Master, does this,

we too are called to touch each other
with love and humility and forgiveness,
washing one another's feet.

If Jesus calls his followers
to wash one another's feet,
to take the last place,
to become like little children,
to be poor in spirit,
to be little, gentle, and humble like him,
to go down the ladder of human promotion,
it is because he knows how quickly
we human beings become attached
to roles, position, and power,
even spiritual power.
He knows how quickly we can use
knowledge and the gifts of God
for our own prestige, honor, and glory
in order to control others.
Pleased with our spiritual selves,
we look into the mirror of self-satisfaction,
closing ourselves up from the God of gifts,
thinking we are the elite of God.

In his gentleness and weakness
Jesus calls us to take the path of service and of humility,
which does not mean that we deny
our gifts, our abilities, and responsibilities.
He reveals that we are called
to receive a new power from God,
the gift of the Spirit,
not for our own glory,
but for the glory of God, the work of God.
This power will allow us to do the impossible:
to live in communion with the poor and the broken,
to be brothers and sisters to all people,
to respect and appreciate
those who are strange or different,

to love our enemies,
to be creative builders of a totally new order:
the Kingdom of Love,
to be a sign in our broken world
of the unity and the love of the Blessed Trinity.

✠

This gift of God,
which transforms us into Jesus,
is given to the little and to the lowly,
to the poor in spirit,
those who cry out their need,
for theirs is the Kingdom of Heaven.
At one moment Jesus exulted in the Spirit
and cried out:

> "Blessed are you, Father,
> Lord of heaven and earth,
> for you have hidden these things
> from the wise and the clever
> and revealed them to the little ones." (Lk 10)

We human beings tend to hide our weaknesses
behind spiritual power and achievements:
We use all our energies to prove we are someone.
We are so thirsty for human affirmation and acclaim,
so frightened of being devalued.
We fall quickly into depression, self-condemnation,
a broken self-image,
angry at our weaknesses, angry at others;
accusing others,
our parents, our community, our society, our Church,
for all the inner pain and helplessness we feel.
But if we recognize and confess our poverty,
our limits and our sinfulness,
and seek also the help and wisdom of others,
if we cry out our needs
to Jesus

and to the Father,
they will give us their gift,
the Holy Spirit,
so that our deepest person
can emerge
in freedom, truth, and humility.
We grow thus to the maturity
of love and compassion,
members of the same body,
in communion one with another.
When weakness is accompanied
by trust, humility, and audacity,
it becomes the way
through which the power of God enters into our being.
The grace of Jesus is manifested
in and through our weakness.

The story of each person is a story of weakness
born and accepted
or rejected in fear and in anger.
We are conceived in weakness,
and we die in weakness.
From weakness we ascend to strength
but then descend again into weakness.
That human story is also the story
of the Word made flesh.

The cry surging from weakness can become,
is called to be,
a cry of love,
opening us up to others
and to God,
not a cry of revolt or despair
surging from our desire to be strong and independent,
which locks us in ourselves.
It is a cry for unity and for compassion
bringing people to oneness and community.
The weakness of another disturbs us

when we want to be left alone
or keep what is *ours.*
But it can also awaken and open our hearts
to communion and to sharing.
When it is welcomed,
weakness becomes communion and sharing;
when it is rejected,
weakness becomes hardness, despair, revolt,
a prelude to death.

We are, of course, called to grow
and to grow in strength and competence,
but this strength is for building up humanity in love,
not for our own glory and power.
We are not called to be independent islands
separated one from another,
closed up in self-satisfaction.
We are all interconnected
interdependent,
called to be one body.
The weak need the strong
just as the strong need the weak
in order not to close up
in suicidal acts of power and pride,
wounding the child within.
The mutual need of hearts is communion.

⌘

To go down the ladder of human promotion
is also to walk into the darkness
at the core of our being
and to make the inner journey into the mud
of our own existence,
into the shadow areas of our own being
from which we hide.
This is the place of emptiness, anguish, and guilt
over which we have created barriers

of self-protection.
There we touch the truth of our inner wounds and flaws,
our fundamental poverty,
and discover how all our so-called good actions
are tainted by the desire for self-glory.
But we touch also
hidden even more deeply within us
the presence of Jesus.
Jesus is present not only in the poor outside us
but in the poor one inside us.

�֍

If the Word became flesh
and lived among the poor, the lowly, and the broken;
if he shared our common humanity
made up of all the mud and dirt and pain of existence,
it was in order to share all his tenderness
with this broken humanity of ours.
He came to draw his followers
along this downward path
to be with the poor, the lame, the crippled, and the blind
to serve them
and to reveal to them their real worth and beauty:
that they are the tabernacle of God,
the light of the world,
the salt of the earth, loved by the Father.
He wanted to reveal to his followers
that the powerless are incredible teachers
and revealers of God.

The cry of the oppressed, the lonely, and the rejected
is essentially a cry
for recognition, presence, and communion.
Their cry disturbs,
creates fear,
provokes rejection.
But if they are listened to,

they can also awaken the hearts
of the powerful and the wise,
calling them to change,
to conversion;
calling them not just to organize and do things
with generosity
but to enter into communion with them.
As the powerful listen to the cry of love
surging up gently from the oppressed and the powerless,
they can begin to accept and love
the vulnerable child within themselves.

That is why Jesus calls his followers
not just to give food to the poor,
the lame, the crippled, and the blind,
but to invite them to their table (Lk 14),
to sit down and eat *with* them,
which means to become their friend,
to receive their gifts and their love,
to empower them with love,
and reveal to them their beauty and value.

And Jesus reveals that he is present,
hidden in the poor, the lame, the blind, and the crippled,
in the rejected and marginalized.

> "Whatsoever you do
> to the least of my brothers and sisters
> you do unto me." (Mt 25)

To feed the hungry is to feed Jesus;
to give water to the thirsty
is to alleviate the thirst of Jesus;
to visit the sick and those in prison
is to visit Jesus;
to welcome a stranger
is to welcome Jesus;
to clothe the naked
is to clothe Jesus.

At one moment Jesus held a little child in his arms
to represent all those who cannot fend for themselves
and said:

> "Whoever welcomes one of these little ones
> in my name,
> welcomes me;
> and whoever welcomes me
> welcomes the one who sent me." (Lk 9)

We must not, however, idealize the poor and the weak
with all their wounds.
Sometimes it can be very painful to be with them
in all their anguish
just as it was painful
to remain close to the crucified Jesus.
The cry of the poor disturbs and shatters security
and carefully planned ways, habits, and social values.
The poor can create dis-order,
crying out for a new order.
The poor and the weak prune, purify.
In their poverty and weakness they reveal
the poverty and weakness,
the darkness and shadow areas
in those with power, comfort, and security
and lead them into insecurity and poverty of spirit.
So it is that the Spirit of Jesus
through all the pain and disturbance
leads us to something new,
a form of chaos
from which is gradually born
a new love
flowing from the heart of God.

The poor and the weak
are gentle prophets
but also disturbing
and wounding prophets.

The Word became flesh
to reveal to us
that the essential work of God
is love;
that the essential work of those who follow his call
is to love people.
This is our joy and our pain,
for love is a gentle master,
a place of ecstasy and communion
but also of pain and crucifixion.

We human beings want so much to *produce* things,
to see results,
to prove our goodness.
But love is never for results;
it is a gift, a free gift.
It is not easy to feel ineffectual,
unable to produce,
with nothing to show for our work,
no affirmation or praise.
It is not easy just to be and to love and to serve.
There is no glory in that.
Yet that is the path of the Word made flesh,
the path that secretly builds community
and humanity.
Jesus calls his followers
to take the downward path,
not just for social action
but in order to live a communion of love
with Jesus
present in the weak and the poor.
This communion flows into silence
and contemplation.
He reveals that as we meet the powerless
and enter into a loving relationship with them
we enter into a loving relationship
with God.

The poor become a sacrament of Jesus,
a place where Jesus resides.
We discover that those who have been rejected
become healers of the heart,
the stone thrown away by the builders
becomes the cornerstone of the new building of God (Mt 2).

The Flesh of Pain

The Word became flesh
to give a new dimension to pain and suffering.
Flesh involves pain
because it is weak and vulnerable,
because death is inscribed in the body
from the moment of its conception.
The Word became flesh
and assumed the limits, the constraints,
and the suffering of flesh.
He went into the very pit of pain,
total, utter rejection,
crying abandonment by God
and abandonment to God.

The logic of love is to love to the very end,
even when there is rejection.
To love is to give oneself.
Is it really love
if one turns away when love is refused?
If one loves
one continues to knock at the locked door
accepting to give one's life
for the loved one.
Jesus accepted to enter that pit of rejection.
By becoming the damned one,
cut off from the religious people,
he brought the loving presence of God
into that very pit.

Condemned by the religious leaders
he brings God to all the so-called damned
of our earth
throughout all ages.
He brings his presence
to all those who feel rejected and abandoned
by the God of religion.

The God of Love did not eliminate pain
nor explain it;
God became one with pain
to reveal his presence to all people
who are in pain
at all times.

The Jesus who cried out:

> "My God, my God,
> why have you abandoned me?"

is the same Jesus who said:

> "He who sees me sees the Father."

The crucified face of Jesus
is also the crucified face of the Father.

Jesus came to reveal that all the pain of the world
has a meaning.
As Jesus gave his life
in pain,
in that ultimate cry of surrender to the Father,
in his death
he gave life;
he transformed the violence he received
into tenderness and forgiveness.
His cry of death
broke down the barriers;
the waters began to flow;
the doors of hearts were unlocked;
the Spirit now flows upon humanity.

With Jesus
all pain, all loss, all rejection, all anguish
can be offered to the Father in sacrifice
and reveal love;
all that is broken
can become fruitful, a source of life,
a gift for others.
Jesus is hidden in pain;
pain thus becomes a sacrament:
the place where Jesus abides.

That does not mean, of course,
that we glorify pain.
We should do all we can to eliminate it.
We are called to be competent
and to struggle against all the forces of evil
that cause pain.
But we must learn also
to be present to people in pain.
Pain is not the ultimate evil
to be shunned.
We must not flee it
or be overcome by it.
Those who flee pain
flee people.
Once we have done everything we can
to eliminate pain,
we are called to accept it,
to walk with it,
and even more
to discover that it can be transformed
by love
into sacrament,
a gift that brings life.

But deeper and more total than the new order of love,
more fundamental even than the offering of pain,
Jesus comes to call his followers

into an ecstasy of love,
the ecstasy of love
that he is living with the Father
before all time.
He comes to offer them this love
through communion with and in his flesh.
He comes to reveal that in the beginning and in the end
is the Wedding Feast.

The Word Who Became Flesh
Invites All to the Wedding Feast

> In the beginning was the Word
> and the Word was *towards* God
> and the Word was God.

John begins his Gospel
in contemplation of the inner life of God.
I have translated *pros ton thēon* as "towards God."
"With" God is clearly accurate,
but I prefer the other possible translation,
which reveals the movement of the Word *towards* God,
in love with God,
totally orientated towards God.

We have already seen how the analogy
of Father and Son
attributed to the inner life of God
has to be completed by another analogy
that reveals another aspect of the life of God.
The Son is from the Father,
flowing from the Father,
and he is clearly in love with the Father,
giving himself to the Father,
one, totally one with the Father.
The being of the Son,
equal in all things with the Father,
is totally *for* the Father.

They are in communion one with another,
in love one with the other.
The love of the one for the other is so total,
so complete,
that this love constitutes the Third Person
of the Blessed Trinity,
the Holy Spirit.
She is the Paraclete.

All creation flows from this life of the Trinity,
the total gift of each person to the other,
the communion between them.
It is this eternal unity and love
that is the beginning and the end
of all things.

All creation is marked by this eternal love of the Trinity,
the to-and-fro of love
between the Father and the Son.
All our immense, beautiful universe sings love,
as each created reality gives and receives
in order that all be held
in unity and harmony.

The Word became flesh
to communicate to us human beings
caught in all the mud, the pain, the fears
and the brokenness of existence,
the life, the joy, the communion,
the ecstatic gift of love
that is the source of all love and life and unity
in our universe
and that is the very life of God.
The Word did not take on flesh
as a garment to be discarded later,
but flesh becomes divine;
it is the medium through which this life of love,
of God,

in God,
is communicated.
This life is not an idea to be learned
through books or teaching;
it is the presence of one person to another,
the gift, the total gift of one to another,
heart to heart,
communion in love.

The Word became flesh
in order to live this communion with each one of us,
a kiss of love
communicating life,
bringing us into the relationship of love
that he has with the Father
and which constitutes his very being.

In communion with Jesus,
one with him, Son of the Father,
proceeding from the Father,
we become in every way children of the Father,
one with the Father, proceeding from the Father.

Jesus said to his disciples:

>"As the Father loves me
>I love you."

The love of the Father
flows into the Son
and from his heart
this love flows
into the heart of each human being
who trusts him.
Through this gift
we live the very life of God;
we participate in the very nature of the Trinity.
Jesus prayed to the Father

"that the love by which you love me
may be in them
and I in them." (Jn 17)

Each one of us is invited
into this eternal wedding feast of love.

"If you only knew the gift of God,"
said Jesus to the woman of Samaria. (Jn 4)

This is his gift of love
given to us in the Holy Spirit.
Jesus came to make all things new.

✵

The Word became flesh,
became weakness,
first of all to enter into communion with the woman,
with Mary,
called by God
to become the beloved mother,
image and sign
of the beloved Father.
This was the first relationship
he lived on earth,
which conditioned
all the other relationships he lived,
just as all our relationships
are conditioned
by this primal relationship with our mothers.

The Word became flesh
to reveal the tenderness of God,
not just through words
but through the very weakness of his flesh,
through the cry surging up for touch,
for presence and for communion.
As the child Jesus drank from his mother's breasts
he drank her love and tenderness
and he gave her his love and tenderness.

Through his flesh,
in this gentle communion,
in this to-and-fro of love,
in the mutual play and song and touch and caring,
he gave her the communion
that bonded him to the Father.

Here is his secret,
Mary's secret too:
she was transformed by his love.
His little cry of love
awoke the sources of love within her,
these sources welling up into eternal life
hidden in her woman's body.
Through the gentle call flowing from his flesh
he led Mary into the mystery
— lived in the littleness of faith —
of the relationship between
the Word and God,
the Son and the Father.
The love of Jesus for Mary
and her love for him
flowed from the heart of the Trinity;
their oneness flowed from the oneness
of the Trinity.
They were one
just as Jesus and his Father are one.

And this oneness was revealed more totally
as she stood by Jesus
crucified and dishonored.
She remains there
in communion with him.
Woman of compassion.

Mary was the first
to live this life of love
directly with God made flesh.

She lived in union with God,
was one with God,
was impregnated by the life and love of God
as no other mystic.
For she lived her life of love
through her flesh,
in ecstasy and in pain,
with the Word made flesh.

That is why Mary,
among all the saints,
throughout all ages,
has a special and unique place of love
in the heart of the Church.
She is, as Elizabeth cried out,
"Blessed among all women."
Yes, all generations will call her blessed.

To love Mary is not then to put her on a pious pedestal,
but to be led by her
to this communion with Jesus
and with his Father,
to all that Jesus asks of us (Jn 3)
and to be present
at the foot of the cross
of those who are crucified today.
Woman of compassion:
she is a gentle model.

⌘

It is this life of love and of light,
this communion of love,
that the Word made flesh gave to Mary,
which is given to us human beings,
according to our call
and in the degree that we put our trust
in Jesus.

The essence of his message
is not to do things,
not even to do things for God,
but to live in communion with him,
to abide in him.
And to be in communion with Jesus
is to be in communion with God,
to be one with God,
in trust.

As Jesus gave his flesh
as the secret instrument of love
for Mary
so too through the Church
he gives his flesh to be eaten,
his blood to be drunk,
so that all who eat and drink thus
live in him
and he in them.
So too he gives his words
that reveal his love and life.
In his words of love
we live in communion with him
and thus with the Father.

In communion with Jesus
we are inspired by the Holy Spirit.
It is no longer we who speak,
but the Holy Spirit in us.
It is no longer we who live,
but Jesus in us.
Jesus came to make all things new.
In communion with him
in the Holy Spirit
we too make all things new
and can do even greater things
than Jesus (Jn 14).

In communion with Jesus,
our actions flow from communion
and are for communion;
our words too are called to flow
from the silence of communion
and lead into the silence of love.
We are called to drink from the heart of Christ
in order to become a source of life for others,
to give our life to others:

>   "As the Father loves me,
>   I love you.
>   My commandment is that you love one another
>   as I love you." (Jn 15)

>   "Let him who thirsts come to me
>   to drink;
>   he who believes in me, as Scripture says,
>   rivers of living waters
>   will flow from his belly." (Jn 7)

This is the ultimate revelation
that Jesus gives to the woman of Samaria.

>   "The waters that I will give to drink
>   will become in you
>   a spring of water
>   welling up into eternal life." (Jn 4)

Transformed in Jesus
we are called to drink from the well of life
hidden in the hearts of each other.

❀

In the book of Revelation
John saw in a vision
the life of the Trinity
in all glory
being communicated through Jesus
to humanity,
to the Church,

to the bride,
to all who are saved:

> "Let us be glad and joyful
> and give glory to God,
> because this is the time
> for the marriage of the Lamb.
> His bride is ready,
> and she has been able to dress herself
> in dazzling white linen.
> Blessed are those invited
> to the wedding feast of the Lamb." (Rev 19)

> "I saw the holy city, the new Jerusalem,
> coming down out of heaven from God,
> prepared as a bride dressed for her husband.
> Then I heard a loud voice call from the throne,
> 'Look, here God lives among human beings.
> He will make his home among them;
> they will be his people and he will be their God,
> God-with-them.
> He will wipe away all tears from their eyes;
> there will be no more death,
> and no more mourning or sadness or pain.
> The world of the past has gone.'" (Rev 21)

> "Come," said one of the angels
> "and I will show you the bride,
> the Spouse of the Lamb." (Rev 21)

This is the end of all things
as humanity participates
in the glory,
the love,
and the life
of the Trinity.
This is the Wedding Feast
to which we are all called.

✖

John called Jesus
the Bridegroom,
revealing as we have already seen
that he is the one
who came to fulfill
the promise of God,
the Lover,
the Bridegroom of Israel,
the beloved one
coming to fill and to fulfill the bride.

Jesus affirms that the Kingdom of God
is like a wedding feast (Mt 22)
at which the poor and the weak
are the special guests.

At a wedding feast in Cana (Jn 2),
at Mary's instigation,
Jesus performed a miracle
and changed water into wine.
John tells us that this was
the "first" sign of Jesus.
The word "first," *archē* in Greek,
means not just the first in time,
but in quality and in value.
The translation could be the "archsign"
as we say archbishop, archetype.
The wedding feast is the fullest of all signs.
It reveals our ultimate destiny as human beings.
We are called to be transformed
as water into wine
and thus to enter into the celebration
of love, of unity, and of glory,
of the blessed Trinity,
not as spectators or on-lookers with cameras,
not as adorers, from afar,
but as the main participants,
as bride and bridegroom

in the ecstasy of gift
and of communion,
in the ecstasy of love
and of life.

In the beginning is the Wedding Feast
of the Trinity.
In the end is the Wedding Feast
of the Trinity.

At the end of time,
humanity,
crushed by wars and catastrophes,
and inwardly broken,
as moral and religious reference points
and barriers disappear,
humanity will cry out from the pits
of loneliness, anguish, and despair
for love and communion.

Or else it will close itself up
in a world
of folly
and of violence.

The Son of Man will then return
upon the clouds
responding to the deep cry of humanity.
Jesus will appear
through the terrifying cracks
of our broken, chaotic world
as a smile of love,
an innocent child,
the Beloved,
rising through the darkness
as the early sun of the day
to enfold each person
in the embrace of love.

Scripture reveals the final cry of humanity:
>   The Spirit and the Bride cry,
>   "Come!" (Rev 22)

The bride, wounded by love,
her flesh agonizing for love,
cries out her thirst for love and presence,
the presence of the Beloved,
the Bridegroom,
to receive his love
and to give herself to him
in love.

>   "Come,
>   come, Lord Jesus, Come."

✿

Here we touch the ultimate meaning
of the Word made flesh
and of all human flesh.
It is the very weakness
and vulnerability
of our flesh
that calls forth love
and transmits love.

The Word became flesh,
became weak,
so that his very weakness,
his broken flesh
would give love and life,
eternal life,
nourishment for all.
Jesus came to transform weakness
from something to be shunned
into a gift,
a call for communion,
awakening and drawing out compassion,
opening hearts,

revealing light.
He came to transform weakness and flesh
into sacrament,
the place where God resides.

The Word made flesh reveals
the mystery and significance
of all human flesh.
The human flesh of man and woman
cleansed
and healed
and uplifted
by the Word made flesh,
was created to be a perfect, wonderful instrument
of love,
and of compassion,
a channel
and a revelation
of the love
that flows in the Heart of the Trinity.
Our flesh is not the painful prison
of our spirit and our mind,
searching to touch a God
separated from our world and from matter
and from all that is limited and finite.
Our flesh is not for the contemplation
of our own beauty,
a beauty that attracts and seduces.
Our flesh is not for our own excitement and pleasure,
which pass and leave renewed emptiness.
Our flesh is not to prove our superiority and power
in the competition of life,
resulting in wars and oppression.
Yes, our bodies are to be developed to the full
in all their beauty and potential,
but not for personal glory and power,
or for that of a particular group.

Our bodies are for communion,
and for the gift of self,
for the unity of all humanity,
which finds its source
in the Word made flesh,
drawing all human hearts
to the unity of communion,
in trust,
in truth,
and in tenderness.

Flesh is for the abiding God,
to become the home of God.
The flesh of Jesus
is the Temple of God.
Our flesh too is the Temple of God.
From this Temple
rivers of living water are called to flow
upon others,
nourishing,
healing,
revealing love and compassion.
Transfigured by the Word made flesh
our flesh becomes a gentle instrument
of the love of God
to flow in others.
This flesh of ours is then no longer a hindrance
to communion with the Word made flesh
and with the Father.
As for Mary
the flesh of Christ,
his humanity,
is the way through which and in which
we meet God.
We are not called to leave the humanity of Christ
in order to meet a God transcending flesh,
but to discover and live

the flesh of Jesus as the flesh of God,
his body as sacrament
to reveal a new meaning to our human flesh:
to reveal to us
the eternal love of the Trinity
where the Father and the Son
in the unity of the Holy Spirit
are in love with one another.

Our bodies are conceived
in silence
and in love;
our first relationship with our mother
is one of communion,
of love through touch
and the weakness of flesh.
We are called to grow, develop,
become competent,
and struggle for peace and justice,
but finally all is for the gift of ourselves,
and for the rest and celebration
of communion.

In the beginning is communion
and in the end is communion.

In the beginning is the Wedding Feast
and in the end is the Wedding Feast
where we give ourselves
in love.